WORK ON PURPOSE

AN ECHOING GREEN PUBLICATION

LARA GALINSKY WITH KELLY NUXOLL
FOREWORD BY LANCE ARMSTRONG AND DOUG ULMAN
AFTERWORD BY GEOFFREY CANADA

Photography by Tony Deifell

Echoing Green
Email: workonpurpose@echoinggreen.org
Tel: (212) 689-1165

First Edition

Additional photographs:
(l-left; r-right)
P. 1: Elizabeth Kreutz/www.elizabethkreutz.com, courtesy of LIVE**STRONG**; p. 3: (l) Elizabeth Kreutz/www.elizabethkreutz.com and (r) Matt Lankes, courtesy of LIVE**STRONG**; p. 28: courtesy of Mel and Pat Oakes; p. 32: courtesy of Nin and Houng Poeuv; p. 57: courtesy of One Acre Fund; p. 84: courtesy of One Acre Fund; p. 86: courtesy of Echoing Green; p. 89: Mark Lotwis, courtesy of Save Darfur Coalition; p. 96: courtesy of Khmer Legacies; p. 101: courtesy of Harlem Children's Zone; p. 103: Patricia Lanza, courtesy of Harlem Children's Zone.

wdydwyd? Registered Trademark 2008

ISBN-13: 978-0-615-41946-6

CONTENTS

Dedicated to the memory of Echoing Green Fellow David Lewis,
whose life story embodies the power of heart, head, and hustle.

· ·

"For all that has been, thanks. For all that will be, yes."
—Dag Hammarskjöld

FOREWORD

We didn't ask for cancer. Nobody does. But when faced with the disease, we saw in ourselves the tenacity to wring some good from a very bad situation. We founded **LIVESTRONG** in 1997 because we wanted to help people who were experiencing the fear, confusion, and isolation that come with a cancer diagnosis. Those feelings were debilitating for us when we had cancer, but sharing them with others helped us to overcome them.

Lance Armstrong and Doug Ulman, LIVE**STRONG**

When we were diagnosed as young athletes at the top of our physical game, we declared ourselves not cancer victims but cancer fighters. We both took active roles in educating ourselves about the disease and the treatment. As a result, we established our own foundations to advocate for others suffering from cancer before we even knew our own fates. And as we helped people, we were continuously encouraged to do even more. Knowing the good we wanted to achieve was the first step.

Every day, we are energized in our mission by stories we hear from cancer survivors—stories both uplifting and heartbreaking. The more we recognize our ability and imperative to effect change, the less willing we are to live with the status quo. We now offer critical support to people living with cancer. We fund patient programs and medical research, initiate advocacy outreach to remind elected officials of the need for favorable policy, and ultimately empower people all over the world to "LIVE**STRONG**."

What will your impact be? There is no shortage of people and causes that need and deserve attention. And there is no limit to what people can accomplish when they approach challenges with both passion and practicality. *Work on Purpose* can be a partner in your efforts, helping you to identify the practical aspects of your mission while encouraging you to pursue your goals.

We all have an obligation to bring positive change to our communities and our world. Fulfilling that obligation requires the boldness not only to envision a better world, but also to recognize your ability to make that world a reality. *Work on Purpose* offers a framework to get started. The vision is all yours.

We wish you all the best in your efforts,

Lance Armstrong

Doug Ulman

LANCE ARMSTRONG is the chairman and founder of LIVE**STRONG**, a global organization fighting for the 28 million people around the world living with cancer today. LIVE**STRONG**'s mission is to inspire and empower anyone affected by cancer. Lance Armstrong won cycling's most prestigious race, the Tour de France, a record-breaking seven times after surviving testicular cancer.

DOUG ULMAN is a three-time cancer survivor and nationally recognized cancer advocate. In his role as president and CEO, Doug is ultimately responsible for the strategic vision and direction of LIVE**STRONG**. After overcoming bone and skin cancer twice during his sophomore year in college, Doug and his family founded the Ulman Cancer Fund for Young Adults, a nonprofit organization to provide support, education, and resources to young adults and their families and friends who are affected by cancer. He served as executive director of the Ulman Cancer Fund for four years before joining LIVE**STRONG**.

INTRODUCTION

When You Grow Up

"What do you want to be when you grow up?"

When I was a kid, I loved answering this question. I'd say I wanted to be a teacher, a veterinarian, or a novelist. Adults would smile, nod in approval, and say, "Your parents must be proud."

Lara Galinsky, Echoing Green

But when I was a senior in college, this was the question I dreaded. It was a constant reminder that I had big decisions to make. I felt immense pressure to be fully in control, 100 percent certain of my goals, and in possession of a detailed, logical plan for my career path. Yet I didn't even know where to start.

What do you want to be when you grow up?

For many of us, it's a question that never really goes away. We are continually searching for what's next, what's better, and what will be even more fulfilling. Even now, in a career I adore and a role that continues to challenge me, I find myself wondering, *how have I landed here?* And yet, *what more can I do?* It's what's underneath this question that's important. That is: *What impact do you want to have on the world?*

The Job Search

As a college senior, I knew I wanted to make a difference—and for me, that meant working in the nonprofit sector. The career resource staff gave me the contact information of alumni who worked in the field; beyond that, they didn't know how to help me. Unfulfilled,

I designed my own process. I pored through entry-level nonprofit job listings and assessed the ones that jumped out at me by evaluating them against a list of the qualities and qualifications I wanted to draw on in my work: youth-focused, a flair for entrepreneurship, a desire to learn on the job, an opportunity to write, and an interest in new technology. I didn't have the language for it then, but I was aligning what I cared about deeply with what I perceived were my best skills.

I followed my own process, and, as with all worthy struggles, it took some time to see results. I didn't find a job, in fact, until many long, harrowing months after I graduated, and that first job wasn't exactly off the charts. The salary was terrible, and I didn't have as much responsibility as I wanted. But I'd come to know myself quite well through my search process, as it helped me understand what I wanted out of my career: to work for an organization that merged talent identification, social change, and entrepreneurship. So I kept looking, going on informational interviews, pushing forward, and searching for opportunities; within a year, I landed at an organization called Do Something and launched an award program that honors young community activists. It felt right for me.

Echoing Green

Now, fifteen years later, I help lead the global nonprofit Echoing Green. We unleash next generation talent to solve the world's biggest problems. Echoing Green helps foster the ecosystem of change-making by providing seed funding, leadership support, and technical assistance to the world's most extraordinary social entrepreneurs and their breakthrough ideas.

Echoing Green is considered a pioneer in the social entrepreneurship movement. Launched in 1987 by the leadership of a private equity firm, General Atlantic, our founders wanted to use proven business principles to effect positive social change. Since its inception, we've invested in 500 social entrepreneurs through our Fellowship program. In turn, our Fellows have launched groundbreaking organizations in over forty-two countries, working on issues as varied as human rights, education, economic development, and housing. While you may not know the name Echoing Green, you've probably heard of the organizations we've helped launch, which include Teach For America, City Year, SKS Microfinance, Share Our Strength, College Summit, Public Allies, the Global Fund for Children, and hundreds more.

In my role at Echoing Green, I help support entrepreneurs with the "know-how" and drive to make a difference—a population of leaders who show us all that we can live up to our greatest potential. All of our Fellows were compelled by a conviction that grabbed them tight and inspired them to make a bold decision to create something new. By the time I met them, the Fellows had already gone through the experience of figuring out what mattered to them and how they wanted to show up in the world. Their clarity of purpose was inspiring.

Over the last five years, I have studied the Fellows' career trajectories. Some of them initially set off down a dissatisfying road and were left unfulfilled; others, like me, had a sense of the professional direction they wanted to take but didn't know how or where to begin. Our Fellows have followed wonderfully varied paths. They come from diverse racial, ethnic, economic, and religious backgrounds. They feel passionate about very different social issues. Yet, there are some remarkable commonalities in how they made the choice to be changemakers.

Heart + Head = Hustle

I learned that all of our Fellows found fulfillment and success when they figured out how to align their hearts and their heads. I have come to believe that all those who build meaningful careers in social change have—whether consciously or unconsciously—synced what they feel strongly about with what they are good at. This alignment produces great impact.

This is it: *Heart + Head = Hustle.*

There is no complex instruction manual to follow, nor a particular academic degree to earn. No targeted experience is required, and certainly no specific suite of skills needs to be developed immediately. It is a simple, powerful formula that can change not only your life but—if you dream big enough—the world around you. By *heart,* I mean your emotions. To figure out where your heart lies, note your own reactions to the world around you. Pay attention whenever you feel love, empathy, anger, a thirst for justice—essentially, any strong emotion. Instead of telling yourself that you're overreacting, or being too "emotional," ask yourself whether you're feeling strongly because you've found a social issue, organization, or role that resonates with you. When you privilege your heart, you'll learn about yourself and what moves you.

By *head,* I mean what you think, your natural skills and abilities, and what you can offer to the world. Your head is the repository for what you learn in school, what you learn on the job, and all your best strategic thinking.

Finding a career that draws on your knowledge and abilities is important, but doing work that fulfills the needs of your heart is equally crucial. If you sync your heart with your head as you make career choices, you'll achieve hustle. I define *hustle* as a state of being "in the zone"— impact-driven and heading toward change. Hustle mode is about being effective, purposeful, and satisfied, because you have found the path that works best for you.

Heart + head = hustle is a framework that changes as you change. The more self-aware you are, the bigger the payoff. If you don't have all the answers now, that's alright. Experiment with this formula. It may take time for you to discover the passions that power your heart and the abilities that guide your head. Keep working with it. The self-knowledge you will gain as you take this process seriously will be a tremendous gift.

All of the Echoing Green Fellows lined up their hearts and their heads when making the decision to start a new organization. Now that they've launched their organizations, they are definitely in hustle mode—intent on moving forward, overcoming obstacles, and turning road-blocks into opportunities along the way.

But for most of the Fellows, heart, head, and hustle took time to achieve. Like me with my first job, they stumbled and suffered through ill-fitting roles. They had to shed old identities and others' expectations to chart their own courses. It took great courage—and even greater self-awareness—to leave behind those unfulfilling paths, but when they did, they were able to find their way to significant personal satisfaction and greater impact.

In this book, you will meet five Echoing Green Fellows and read about their experiences aligning their hearts with their heads to achieve personal fulfillment and societal impact. As you read, you'll see that their paths were very different. They struggled at different times in very different ways. Yet now they stand before the world as changemakers, just as you can.

Your Path to Boldness

If you want to craft a meaningful career, this book is for you. If you don't know what to do professionally but enjoy being helpful to others, this book is for you. If you are about to graduate from college and are overwhelmed by the notion of finding your first job, this book is for you. If you are feeling pressure to live out someone else's dream, this book is for you. If you are in your first job but feel lost, this book is also for you. If you are happy with your place in the social sector but want to continue to strive for even more impact and meaning, once again, this book is for you.

You may see your own life in the stories of Andrew, Cheryl, Mark, Mardie, and Socheata, the five Echoing Green Fellows profiled here. But even if you don't, I hope this book allows you to reflect on what you want: *What social footprint do you want to make? What is your problem to own? What gifts do you have to offer to the world? What path do you want to take?*

In a way, these difficult but important questions are what underlie that initial inquiry from childhood, *What do you want to be when you grow up?* I've found an answer now, and not just because I love my job. Rather, I've discovered that the truest answer I can give is one I share with the five Echoing Green Fellows profiled here, and hopefully with you, too. When I grow up, I want to be a change-maker. If this resonates, you are in the right place. Keep reading.

CHAPTER 1
WHERE IT ALL BEGINS

As someone who was once a job seeker relying on the kindness of people willing to help steer me in the right direction, I've made a commitment to assist people who want impact-driven careers. Over the years I've advised hundreds of people getting started in the working world or thinking about changing careers. Many of them were floundering. They'd taken internships, jobs, and professional paths that didn't suit them. It took all the strength they could muster to admit they disliked what they were doing. And then they faced the even more difficult challenge of figuring out what they did want to do.

As I've talked to these career seekers, I've been struck by similarities in what they say. Most know what they don't want to do. They have learned this the hard way, through making mistakes, taking jobs that made them miserable, or following someone else's path instead of their own.

Furthermore, most have only a vague sense, if any at all, of what they *do* want to do. I hear, "I want to make a difference" or "I want to help people" or "I know I do NOT want to work in investment banking anymore."

Sometimes career seekers do have a more focused plan. They'll say, for example, "I want to work in international economic development" or "I'm interested in microfinance." When I dig deeper and ask "why" questions (*Why does microfinance interest you? Why do you want a career focused on making*

a difference?), there are long pauses. I know that these questions are difficult. After all, it's much easier, and much more common, to ask "what," "when," and "where" questions (*What did you like about your last job? When did you graduate from college? Where do you want to live?*). But, the "why" question cuts to the heart of what drives you. When the Echoing Green team and I gather new Fellows each year, they share stories answering, "Why do you do what you do?"

Instead of posing familiar questions, I ask people to go all the way back to their childhoods and try to identify clues that could reveal a way forward. It's often a challenging exercise. Few people have thought about how their upbringings, communities, and pivotal life experiences relate to their career paths. Yet the events and people that made the biggest impression on us growing up don't go away when we start our professional lives. The stories of many changemakers suggest that the convictions and values forged in childhood are a *foundation* for a career with personal and social meaning. In this book, you'll meet people who didn't know they were headed toward careers as changemakers.

Yet when you read about their pasts in the following pages, you'll be able to see exactly where their "why" comes from.

ANDREW
HELP ALL WHO ARE SUFFERING

Andrew Youn grew up hearing two clear messages in his home: Try hard to succeed, and help those in need.

His parents modeled both values. Mr. and Mrs. Youn had moved from Korea to the United States, where they met as graduate students at the University of Minnesota. Andrew and his brother were raised in Minneapolis, in a narrow, two-bedroom apartment outfitted with secondhand furniture. As a kid, Andrew came home from school and did homework alongside his parents – his mother had recently received her Ph.D. in mathematics, and his father was fresh out of architecture school. When they took a break for dinner, the Youns always said the same prayer: "Help all the people in the world, especially those who are suffering.

Andrew observed that his parents practice what they prayed. While in graduate school, on the last day of the month, Mrs. Youn sat down at the Formica kitchen table and wrote a check for $100—half her graduate student stipend—to her parents and siblings in Korea, who shared an apartment and had only intermittent access to running water. When Andrew thought about his cousins trying to do their homework

in a cold, crowded room, he was grateful for how easy things were for him in comparison. He might be an underdog in the United States, a shy kid with glasses who wasn't perfectly fluent in American culture, but at least he was warm, well fed, and getting a good education.

The combination of his parents' example and his own gratitude inspired Andrew to help others, too. In elementary school, he visited people at a homeless shelter, played soccer with kids in low-income neighborhoods, served Thanksgiving dinners, and collected canned goods. By age thirteen, he was doing community service every week. His school had a community service requirement, and most of his friends did some service work, too, but Andrew's enthusiasm was voracious. While other kids his age enjoyed computers, sports, or music, Andrew loved providing relief to people in need.

When Andrew was a junior in high school, he had an experience that made him wonder if he could turn his passion for service into his profession. His church group went to Mexico to build houses. He had used all his savings to pay for the trip, and by the time he arrived in the small town where his group was working, he

had only enough cash to pay for the meals he'd eat during the trip.

While the rest of the group moved quickly to the building site, Andrew dawdled behind. As he took in the sights of the tin-roofed houses, the dusty streets, and the dogs panting in the heat, a woman with a baby stepped in his path and begged him for food. Her child's arms were no thicker than a doll's, and the fatigue in her eyes made Andrew think that her request had already been turned down many times that day. He fumbled in his pocket and handed her five dollars. It was his lunch money, but the smile the woman flashed made

Andrew's small sacrifice worth it. Giving his money to someone who needed it was a lot more satisfying than buying a sandwich, he decided. In that moment on the street, Andrew felt useful. He wondered if he could find a way to feel so useful every day of his life.

• • •

For college, Andrew went to Yale on a hefty financial aid package. Approaching higher education as an opportunity to undertake a serious study in how to do good, he joined the campus volunteering center and found work-study jobs with

15

nonprofits or campus groups that served those in need.

By his junior year, Andrew was devoting over twenty hours a week to socially-focused projects. After class and on the weekends he stocked shelves at a food pantry, wrote letters to Congress on behalf of a children's advocacy organization, built more houses, and researched food security for the government. However, he was beginning to wonder whether his efforts were useful. Yes, he realized he could improve someone's immediate circumstances by providing a meal or a roof, and that eventually legislation could have a long-lasting impact. However, Andrew rarely saw how his manual labor or office work affected the larger issues of hunger or homelessness. His effort seemed out of proportion with its impact. Andrew scraped by on a few hours of sleep and seven dollars an hour, and the vast majority of the suffering people in the world continued to struggle.

At the same time, Andrew was learning in his classes how money flowed through society, leaving some people with more wealth and resources than others. In one memorable economics lecture, a professor described two men stranded on a desert island. One man had two shirts, and the other had two pairs of pants. The professor pointed out that neither had to give away everything he had for each one to be fully dressed. Instead, the two men could trade. The scenario was a classic description of a market economy. Capital, savings, technology, and investments are the tools people needed to participate in a market economy and develop long-term resources.

Inspired by this thinking, Andrew offered to find a job for a homeless man he'd come to know. A stable income would be more valuable to this man than a few one-off donations, Andrew reasoned. He asked local restaurants and bars if they had any openings for dishwashers or bar backs. Employers were reluctant. Andrew insisted that his friend would be a good hire—all he needed was a chance. Finally, one of the managers relented and said yes as a favor to Andrew. At last, he'd made a real, long-term difference in someone's life. Andrew was thrilled. He raced to the park and told his friend the good news.

But two weeks later, when Andrew passed by the bar to see how his friend was doing, the manager said the man had come once or twice and then stopped showing up. No one had seen him since.

Andrew felt like an utter failure. He'd let down the bar manager, he hadn't made a difference for his friend, and he'd demonstrated that, despite being smart and well educated, he was incapable of helping one person, let alone many people.

Discouraged and embarrassed, Andrew let go of his teenage fantasy of a career in service. He just didn't believe he could have a real impact. Besides, he didn't know how he could both help those who were suffering and support himself. He set his sights on becoming a math professor or a business consultant working in finance instead. After all, those professions were likely to pro-vide a good income and make use of his knack for numbers.

As a first step, he sent applications to a handful of management consult-ing firms. Consulting would offer him a chance to take all the economic theories he'd been studying and apply them in the real world. He could figure out what really worked and what didn't. The field also offered prestige and a good salary. Consulting positions were competitive,

and Andrew felt flattered and relieved when he was offered one. Gratefully, he said yes.

Yet from the moment he accepted the job, Andrew separated his intellectual gifts from his passion, his head from his heart. Almost immediately, he regretted this division.

CHERYL
ACHIEVEMENT AND UNCERTAINTY

Cheryl Dorsey's parents didn't push her. They didn't tell her she *had* to be or do one thing or another. But as an African American girl who'd been given every opportunity, she thought she owed it to her parents and her community to succeed. And in her worldview, success looked pretty traditional: You became a doctor, lawyer, or engineer.

Her own parents were public school teachers who'd bought a three-story house in the Maryland suburbs in part to give Cheryl, their only child, the best chance for a good education. Education meant everything to Mr. and Mrs. Dorsey. They were among the first in their families to go to college—both attended a historically black university in Baltimore—and they'd devoted their professional lives to helping other young men and women of color achieve higher education.

One of Mr. Dorsey's pupils, who later became a U.S. congressman, told Cheryl that her father taught him what it meant to be an African American professional man. In Mr. Dorsey's classroom, there were no excuses for shirttails being untucked, pants hanging down, or shoes being untied. Mr. Dorsey himself never showed up to his school in anything less formal than a jacket and tie. And he made it clear that if a student's grades weren't up to snuff, Mr. Dorsey expected significant improvements in the next semester. Cheryl's mother's entire career centered on sending low-income students to college and providing them with the same opportunities her own child received. A full-time high school guidance counselor, she also worked part-time at Upward Bound, a federally-funded college access program, to earn extra money for Cheryl's college tuition fund and to steer kids without means to college.

Anytime the phone rang at home, it was likely one of Mrs. Dorsey's students looking for advice and support. They told her about their bad grades, their families' inabilities to make ends meet, their attempts to make their families understand the importance of college, or the fear they felt because there was no money, no food, no shelter, or no safety. Mrs. Dorsey helped her students navigate life's barriers, some self-imposed and some thrust on them by external forces. But like her husband, Mrs. Dorsey never lowered her expectations.

Growing up, Cheryl absorbed her parents' teaching. She learned to hold herself to high standards and to make

opportunities for others even as she strived for her own success. Most importantly, she learned about injustice. Both her parents believed that injustice was a given—society discriminated based on class, gender, and race—but they also believed that injustice was not an excuse. Mr. and Mrs. Dorsey taught all the young people in their lives, including Cheryl, to use intelligence and education to get ahead in an unfair world.

• • •

Mr. and Mrs. Dorsey's focus on higher education meant that Cheryl's own college matriculation was not just a goal, but also an expectation. Her parents did everything they could to help her prepare for it. When she outgrew summer camp, Cheryl went to a residential program at Cornell; to supplement her regular high school classes, she took calculus at a nearby university.

Yet for all the investment in her educational career, Cheryl had given little critical thought to her professional career. If asked, she said she wanted to be a pediatrician or a veterinarian, because she liked children and animals. Those who couldn't speak up for themselves

19

friendly with students from all cliques but not an obvious geek or jock, and not a natural fit with the artistic or hip crowds. Each day she floated between groups, moving from lunch with her African American friends to honors classes where she was one of few people of color. Her extended family was close and loving, but as an only child whose cousins were either older or younger, she often felt like an outsider separated from those around her by age, class, and experience.

More insidious were Cheryl's grave doubts about her abilities and merit. It was hard for her to believe that she was as intelligent and talented as her parents seemed to think. Her doubts were confirmed when a guidance counselor steered Cheryl, along with a number of other top-performing African American seniors, to mid-tier colleges and universities. Cheryl didn't know what to make of the guidance counselor's advice. Mrs. Dorsey, however, knew exactly what she thought. "You have an opportunity to get the education you want," she told Cheryl one night after dinner. "Don't go back to that counselor. And if she asks, tell her she's not responsible for you anymore. We will handle this on our own."

Over the next few months, Cheryl studied college catalogs with her mother,

struck Cheryl as vulnerable, and she wanted to help them. But she didn't know very much about what a medical career entailed, and she didn't spend a lot of time searching her heart to learn if she truly had a calling to practice medicine.

Cheryl's lack of clarity wasn't unusual for a teenager, but in her case, the confusion she felt prefigured uncertainty that would stay with her well into adulthood. She was plagued by two questions: *Where do I fit in?* and *Am I good enough?*

In high school, Cheryl fit in nowhere and everywhere. She was almost six feet tall, with two long braids, a wide smile, and a big voice—a likeable young woman, wrote draft after draft of essays, and typed responses to application questions, which she checked and double-checked. Throughout the process, Mrs. Dorsey was encouraging and patient. She took what Cheryl saw as an impossible process and made it surmountable. Most important, her assurance made Cheryl feel confident. She felt as if she and her mother were pulling back the curtain and showing her the way into a world she knew little about.

The following spring, Cheryl was accepted to Harvard. Everyone celebrated her. Her teachers and neighbors said they were impressed but not surprised—Cheryl had always been on the path to success. Her extended family was overjoyed. A cousin even told her she was his new favorite status symbol. And Cheryl's parents were so proud they couldn't stop smiling.

The congratulations were heartfelt and well intended. Everyone seemed to believe that Cheryl deserved a great education and the rewards that came with it. But the attention made Cheryl nervous. Now that she was faced with the reality of actually going, she found Harvard's reputation daunting. Her family's praise only made it worse. By the time she packed her bags for Cambridge, she was certain that she would disappoint everyone who was rooting for her.

MORE INSIDIOUS WERE CHERYL'S GRAVE DOUBTS ABOUT HER ABILITIES AND MERITS.

MARK
THE BOOK OF WHY

Mark Hanis says he owes his life to genocide. After all, if it hadn't been for the Holocaust, his grandparents never would have met.

All four of Mark's grandparents fled continental Europe at the start of World War II. Two went to the United Kingdom, the other two to South America. They eventually met, married, and had children. Mark's parents met in the United States and settled in Ecuador—which is how Mark and his sister came to grow up in a Jewish enclave in the middle of a Latin country.

As a child, Mark was constantly reminded of genocide and its effects. He could see it in his family's European faces and hear it in his grandparents' voices. He recognized it in the old people in town, whose concentration camp numbers were tattooed onto their skin. He read it on the stickers pasted on nearly every glass door on the synagogue: "Never Again."

Nevertheless, if someone had asked Mark when he was growing up what he could do about genocide, he probably would have said he had no influence over systematic, deliberate destruction of a group of people. He saw genocide as a phenomenon, not as a problem to be solved. Besides, Mark was more focused on how he could contribute to his immediate community.

Both Mark's school and his faith promoted service and a meaningful life. Like Andrew, Mark had to log volunteer hours in order to graduate from high school. His synagogue also espoused *tikkun olam*: the belief that the world was broken and that human beings could heal it through good deeds, hard work, and observance of the rule of law.

As a student, Mark volunteered for groups that allowed him to work with purpose and effectiveness. In middle school, he joined the Boy Scouts, an organization that encourages community involvement and personal achievement; he also won a seat in student government, where he helped make decisions about resource allocation, identifying which projects were likely to succeed, which were ill conceived, and which were worthy of the school's funds. He rushed between meetings in slacks and a collared shirt, resolute in his tasks and affable with his peers, whom he recruited for projects.

Concern for local children defined Mark's high school years. He was moved by the plight of kids who played in landfills while their parents scavenged for

food. The kids were in physical danger, and their parents were impoverished. Mark realized he couldn't solve either of those large-scale problems; but instead of feeling helpless, he thought of a small way to help. He worked with classmates and teachers to start a day care in his school, giving the children a safe place to play. The project succeeded and showed Mark his own ability to have a positive influence, even in the face of seemingly insurmountable societal problems.

As Mark began to think about his career plans, the families he served at the day care center were never far from

his mind. He thought he might get a law degree and try to improve international trade policies, thereby helping Ecuadorians who were struggling financially. If that didn't work out, he imagined he might become a soldier and defend the interests and lives of his countrymen. Either way, he was drawn to professions that involved protecting people.

Mark's parents shared his enthusiasm for people-centered work. Mrs. Hanis had been a customer service representative for an airline, and Mr. Hanis sold medical equipment. Both Mr. and Mrs. Hanis were excellent communicators, and Mark

economic development at Swarthmore College in Pennsylvania. In Mark's sophomore year, an alumnus told him about an internship with an international war crimes tribunal in Sierra Leone, West Africa. The country had been through ten years of civil war, during which over 50,000 people were killed and tens of thousands displaced.

Mark didn't know much about Sierra Leone, but he recognized that the internship would give him an opportunity to be involved in substantive work. There were hurdles to overcome—accepting the internship would mean taking a semester off from school, and he had to raise several thousand dollars to go. But the work appealed to his concerns for safety and security, and he expected he would learn a lot.

Seven months later, at the end of Mark's internship, the tribunal was a robust operation. It had moved from a single house into permanent headquarters, where lawyers and officials from around the world hurried among a network of trailers. They had organized a comprehensive response to a decade of murder, maiming, and human rights violations. A dozen warlords were slated to come to trial.

Mark felt proud of their work, but he was also indignant. If the international

picked up from them the art of conversation. They taught him how to approach people with respect, articulate what he wanted, and negotiate effectively.

They also cultivated his powers of reason and analysis. As a gift, they gave him *The Jewish Book of Why*. The title made an impression on him with its suggestion that he was allowed, even encouraged, to question things that other people took for granted. He didn't need to accept things as they were—he could investigate them, examine their causes and history, and even seek to change them.

• • •

The drive to change society carried Mark through high school and into university, where he studied political science and community could establish a criminal court in a grassy field in only a few months, why hadn't they intervened when the atrocities were happening? Or before they started?

Being in Africa made Mark palpably aware that mass killings and atrocities weren't aberrations. They happened all the time. They were happening now, in Sierra Leone, in the Congo, and in Sudan. Some of these clashes were already considered genocides. Others were on their way to being defined as genocides. It struck Mark for the first time that he was living in a world where events just like the Holocaust were occurring *every day*, and he wanted to stop them.

Mark returned to the United States full of determination to help stop genocide, but he didn't have any plan to achieve his goal. He lacked a strategy, and his unfocused passion would not only delay his success, but it would also land him in the hospital.

BEING IN AFRICA MADE MARK PALPABLY AWARE THAT MASS KILLINGS AND ATROCITIES WEREN'T ABERRATIONS.

MARDIE
PARADE OF HOMES

In 1972, a presidential election year and the year Mardie Oakes was born, her neighborhood was declared a microcosm of the national population and therefore a political bellwether. "We're so average, we're unaverage," said one of Mardie's neighbors.

Like many other residents in their Austin, Texas neighborhood, the Oakes family was white, middle-class, and Protestant. Many of the neighborhood homes were unremarkable, but Mardie got lots of exposure to different architectural styles. Every year, she went with her parents to the Parade of Homes, an annual Austin event during which new houses—many of them enormous custom homes in suburban developments—were open to the public. And every Sunday, after church, Mardie and her family would take long drives around the city, looking at houses in upscale neighborhoods. Mardie's favorites were the quirky ones—modern with lots of glass or old Victorians full of secret nooks and crannies.

The Oakes's house was plain and practical: a single-story building with peach-colored wood siding, white shutters, and brick accents. Inside, the house had small, square bedrooms with an open floor plan, so there were few places to talk privately or squirrel away unnoticed with a book.

The layout of the house reflected the no-nonsense attitude of its owners. Dr. Oakes was a physics professor who believed that memorizing a formula was no way to learn. Mrs. Oakes was also a teacher, alternating between sixth grade English and social studies. They expected their three daughters to focus on academics. The youngest, Mardie, was allotted thirty minutes of personal time every evening. Outside of that, she was expected to practice her viola and review her studies. It wasn't enough simply to do her homework, jotting down the answers to history review questions or math problems. Each night her father insisted that Mardie sit next to him on the "homework couch," a blue velveteen love seat in the dining room, and explain how she'd arrived at the answers.

Her parents' encouragement, combined with their insistence on doing thorough work, helped Mardie believe she could accomplish something important one day. But she didn't see herself as an educator like her parents. Even as a little girl, she realized that she loved houses. She was fascinated by their engineering and design, and she was

captivated by how they could make a person feel. She knew that one day she wanted to make them.

• • •

When Mardie was in the third grade, the Austin schools were desegregated. At the time, Mrs. Oakes was the president of the Parent Teacher Association (PTA), and she supported the measure. The city's resources were allocated unevenly, she pointed out, and it was only fair to try to bring some equity into the system.

Other parents in the neighborhood may have agreed with Mrs. Oakes's politics, but they didn't want their families to have to make any adjustments. Many of them enrolled their children in private school. Mardie and her sisters stayed in the public system. Under the desegregation agreement, kids from less affluent neighborhoods were bused into Mardie's school. Then, a few years later, the busing switched directions: Every day, Mardie rode a bus for forty-five minutes each way to attend classes with African American and Hispanic students on the other side of town.

Mardie was proud of her mother's courage and commitment to social

As the bus bumped and lurched, Mardie watched as power poles replaced trees, lawns went from lush to barren, and houses narrowed and looked shabbier, but more interesting. In the windows she saw tomato plants and flowers growing out of coffee tins. One family had adorned the front door with a frieze made of rusty bicycle parts. One house was painted a fresh neon green. Mardie wondered what the owner was thinking. *Did she particularly like the color and want to make a statement? Was she trying to irritate her neighbors? Or had she just found the paint on sale?* Whatever the reason, Mardie admired that the owner had made the home uniquely hers, despite the fact that she seemed not to have much money.

• • •

By the time she was a high school kid with bleached blond hair and frosted pink lipstick, Mardie felt welcome in many different kinds of homes. When she was sixteen, she created a particularly strong attachment to one.

On a summer evening, a friend had to back out of a babysitting job at the last minute, and Mardie agreed to take over. She put on her gold jelly shoes and drove a couple of miles to a small, plain-looking

justice, and she enjoyed the friends she made. She liked that they were different than she was. Her new group of friends appealed to her as much as the houses that she observed on the long ride to school.

bungalow. No one answered when she knocked. Mardie turned the doorknob and poked her head inside. Toys and games were strewn all over the wall-to-wall carpet, a brown couch sagged in the living room, and the breakfast dishes were still scattered across a newspaper on the dining room table. Although it looked nothing like her family's tidy ranch house, Mardie—who was always getting in trouble for her messy room—immediately felt at home.

A child squealed, and Mardie followed the sound of his voice through the kitchen and out to the back patio. There, a toddler and a four-year-old were racing around the outside of an inflatable baby pool. Their mother was sitting in the water up to her waist, fully dressed and laughing. Mardie was both shocked and delighted. The family seemed fun loving and impulsive, and she couldn't help but want to be a part of it.

"Hello?" she called out.

All three family members turned around. Without warning, the toddler—Patrick—ran straight into Mardie's arms. Even though he was soaking wet, Mardie didn't jump away. Instead, she wrapped her arms tightly around him, never dreaming she'd spend the next twelve years trying not to let him go.

SHE WRAPPED HER ARMS TIGHTLY AROUND HIM, NEVER DREAMING SHE'D SPEND THE NEXT TWELVE YEARS TRYING NOT TO LET HIM GO.

SOCHEATA
SAFE AND SOUND

Growing up, Socheata Poeuv didn't think much about where she came from. She knew that her parents, her two older sisters, and her older brother had fled Cambodia in 1979 after the Khmer Rouge genocide and that she was born in a refugee camp in Thailand. A few months later, she and her family moved to Dallas, Texas. There, Socheata usually felt like any other girl her age, going to school, doing her homework, and trying to be a good sister and daughter.

That her background as a refugee was unusual didn't occur to her until she was nine years old. During summer vacation, Socheata and her siblings were outside weeding the front lawn. Socheata approached the chore without resistance. They often weeded the lawn on the weekends during the summer. Besides, her parents had taught her that work was a privilege—it passed the time, gave you a goal, earned you a place in society, and offered you a chance to make a contribution. For the Poeuvs, work was almost sacred.

Yet on this day, as Socheata bent over and began plucking out weeds, it struck her that other families around Dallas didn't weed their lawns. They hired gardeners to do it, or, if they were do-it-yourself types, they sprayed weed killer. Socheata assumed none of her classmates were spending their Saturday afternoons jerking up dandelions by the roots.

No sooner did she have the thought than a car horn beeped behind her. She glanced over her shoulder and saw a girl from her class passing in a convertible, red ponytail sailing behind her, tennis racket in the backseat. Socheata was mortified. For the first time, she saw her family through someone else's eyes. She imagined that they must look like a scene from Southeast Asia—four black-haired figures bending over the grass, as if they were in a rice field. It made her realize that her family must seem different, perhaps disadvantaged. The thought sat uncomfortably with Socheata, who didn't think of herself as an immigrant. The car honked again, and the classmate waved and called her name. But instead of standing up to be recognized, Socheata closed her eyes and willed herself to disappear.

• • •

From that time on, she began to notice unusual things about her family. For instance, her parents' relationship sometimes struck her as odd. Mr. and Mrs. Poeuv seemed to have almost nothing in

common. Mrs. Poeuv liked to joke and tell stories. She had a loud, confident voice and asked for what she wanted. Whenever distant relatives arrived from Cambodia, she didn't hesitate to rap on the manager's door of the factory where she worked and introduce her relatives as his new laborers, promising they'd be reliable and industrious.

Mr. Poeuv was also quick to help anyone who needed it, but Socheata thought of him mainly as a sweet follower. He worked a night shift at the factory, which meant he rarely ate a meal with the family. When he was home, he tried to stay out of the way.

As far as Socheata could see, her parents didn't talk with each other. There was no animosity between them, but there were no signs of affection, either. Once, Socheata heard her mother say of her father, "He's a good man." But other than that, Mrs. Poeuv didn't even acknowledge him, except to point out that whenever there was a noise in the middle of the night, *she* was the one who had to investigate.

The fear of noises in the night exemplified something else Socheata noticed about her parents—they were consumed by worry. They didn't allow their children

31

others what to do. Most of the time she sat in the back of the classroom, listening attentively but reluctant to raise her hand unless she had something important to say. At the end of the day she walked directly home, finished her assignments, and then settled in with a book.

Language and stories became her primary friends. She enjoyed getting lost in a book and then thinking about how the narrative had been put together—each word, sentence, paragraph, and chapter fitting together like a puzzle. The books and magazines she read also fueled her curiosity about the world. She imagined traveling one day and reporting on what she saw. Or she'd become a poetry professor, happily ensconced in a university and soaking up all the learning around her. But whatever she did, she expected it to come with a steady paycheck. Her parents had instilled in her that security was the most important ambition of all.

to leave the house alone except on school-related activities, and they didn't let them invite friends over. The Poeuvs' only visitors were the relatives who slept on the couch until Mrs. Poeuv could find them a job or other Cambodian families who came for supper after temple on Saturdays. Hemmed in by her parents' anxiety, Socheata lived a childhood and adolescence limited almost entirely to the Cambodian community.

In part because of her parents' cautious attitude toward outsiders, Socheata felt removed from her peers. At school, she was a diligent student and a polite classmate, but she had no desire for public achievement or popularity. She instinctively distrusted people who called attention to themselves or tried to tell

With that in mind, when it came time to apply for college, Socheata pinned her sights on schools that could help her land a good job. Smith College in Massachusetts, with its excellent reputation and strong alumni network, did the trick. Her parents hated to see her go so far away from home, but she assured them that a Smith degree meant she'd be able to support herself. And, she hoped, help them.

BOLD Qs

WHAT MOMENTS FROM YOUR CHILDHOOD SHAPED WHAT YOU THINK IS IMPORTANT?

CHAPTER 2
LIVES OUT OF WHACK

Although the words and actions we absorb in our homes profoundly shape our ideas of what is important, when it comes time to start a professional life, we often put those early experiences aside. They can be overshadowed by the desire to earn a good salary, the pressure to follow a particular path, and the need to satisfy competing demands from our families, our peers, and ourselves.

Few people fall immediately into jobs or paths that satisfy all these desires, let alone stem from what they think is meaningful. Most people—including all the changemakers in this book—wander or take misguided turns.

They find themselves in situations and roles that don't make sense for them. They are disconnected from the positive influences of their upbringings, or have not yet found a way to release the effects of past challenges—disagreements with parents, conflicts with siblings, trouble fitting in with classmates—whatever held them back and made them unhappy when they were young.

If you've been in a job that left you bored, frustrated, anxious, or unfulfilled, you might identify with some of the stories on the following pages. The struggle is part of finding a career and a life that have purpose—a career and life that make sense uniquely to you, even if they don't make sense to others. It's hard to endure those times when you feel out of whack. But however difficult they are as you're experiencing them, those times are valuable. They can help you step away from a path that's wrong for you and discover one that's just right.

ANDREW
SIXTY:TWO

It was a Monday afternoon in Boston, and Andrew was eating lunch at his desk. Sandwich crumbs fell on his shirt and tie, but he didn't bother to brush them off. No one would see him in his cubicle. Besides, he was preoccupied with watching the clock. Only three more hours to go.

In the cube next to him, another junior analyst typed loudly on his keyboard. Across the aisle, Andrew could hear someone else chattering into the phone. All the people on his floor had joined the consulting firm together after college, but Andrew rarely talked to his cohort anymore. He'd heard all their stories, and since everyone worked sixty hours a week, they didn't have much time to have new experiences worthy of discussion. Andrew preferred to keep to himself.

Shoving the last bite of his sandwich into his mouth and pushing his slipping glasses back on his nose, he tried to focus again on his work. A huge airline company had hired his consulting firm to figure out how to increase its profit margin. Andrew's task was to comb through a database of airplane supply parts and find vendors that would cut a deal for a cheaper price. When he identified a likely candidate, Andrew highlighted it and checked it against another database.

The task struck him as boring. He reminded himself that the consulting firm was teaching him valuable business skills and that it gave him a chance to watch how senior businesspeople made decisions. But nothing changed the fact that he didn't feel passionate about the work he was doing. The lack of a bigger purpose depressed him. His job was to help multibillion-dollar companies earn more money, when his heart was with the millions of people trying to survive on less than a dollar a day.

He also couldn't help but chafe at his role. Just because Andrew had a kind heart didn't mean he didn't also have an ego. He felt underutilized. He wasn't drawing on his analytical ability or his reserves of energy. He felt like a cog in a giant machine, a mechanical part whose only value was to keep things moving. To stay engaged, he multitasked, toggling between making a spreadsheet for the month's work-flow and refereeing an email argument between two summer interns. He would have liked to leave the office, but his boss expected him to find another few million dollars in savings. No matter what he did, Andrew kept coming up short.

• • •

When the clock struck three, Andrew came to life. He jumped up, threw on his suit jacket, and rushed to the elevator. The consulting firm, one of the most socially conscious in the industry, paid for employees to spend a few hours a week volunteering, and Andrew eagerly took them up on the offer. He hoped the Monday afternoons he dedicated to a children's shelter would keep him motivated for the rest of the week. He felt he had a critical mission at the shelter: to make kids laugh.

The kids looked up from their homework as soon as Andrew walked in the door. They were in temporary care while their mothers dried out from alcohol, and their faces looked drawn and anxious, like they'd already been used up by life. Andrew did whatever it took to take their minds off their situation. He cracked jokes, made silly faces, and used goofy voices.

When they finished their homework, he took them to the soccer field. He looked absurd running around in his slacks and tie, but he didn't hold back. He raced after the kids with his arms above his head, whooping and hollering. His hijinks worked: The withdrawn,

In the taxi from the shelter back to the office, Andrew told himself for the thousandth time that it was madness to spend sixty hours a week doing something he didn't enjoy and two hours a week doing what he loved. He knew his heart and head were operating independently—so independently that, despite the best intentions of his boss and colleagues, at work Andrew mostly felt numb. He didn't want to have that sensation for the rest of his life, but he didn't know how to both be of use and do well, and he was reluctant to give up the benefits and prestige of his consulting job.

antisocial kids gradually loosened up, smiled, and started having fun. When they got tired, they collapsed on the grass and made up nonsense rhymes until everyone giggled and shrieked.

In some ways, volunteering was much easier than what he did at the consulting firm; in others, it was more of a challenge. Andrew felt he earned every smile he got. He was proud of his contribution to the shelter. The kids also made him feel human—hopeful and loving, and like he was an important part of their lives. The time he spent with them seemed to matter. But it always seemed too short.

With a sigh, Andrew returned to his cubicle. The floor still hummed as a dozen junior analysts worked. Above their heads, the windows had turned dark. Without saying hello to anyone, Andrew sank into his chair and shook the mouse to wake up his computer. The proposal to the airline company was due by midnight, and to meet the deadline, Andrew would have to start cranking.

As his eyes scanned the database, searching for savings, he could almost hear his heart switch off.

CHERYL
A DEWDROP ON A ROSE PETAL

Cheryl slid on her white coat and adjusted her stethoscope. Her neck tensed at the touch of the metal on her skin, and her chest felt tight beneath the instrument's diaphragm. She wondered how her father had worn a tie to teach school all those years. She couldn't wait to take off the stethoscope at the end of the day. Unfortunately, her days usually didn't end until late in the evening, and she had to be back at the hospital at dawn.

As she crossed the floor of the busy emergency room, Cheryl avoided her fellow residents, who were bantering about weekend plans and trading jokes. She envied their ability to take in stride, even enjoy, the long hours, lack of sleep, and high-pressure nature of medical residency. At the hospital, Cheryl was tired and serious, intent on her work but not inspired by it. Pediatric residency was the final stage before she became a full-fledged physician. Above all else, the residency had taught her that she didn't enjoy clinical medicine. With a sigh, she picked up the next chart in the queue.

The patient was a toddler who'd been crying for two days. He hadn't been sleeping, his mother said. She thought he was running a fever.

With her slender hands and low, gentle voice, Cheryl kept the child calm while she examined his heart, lungs, ears, eyes, and throat. She was confident that this was yet another typical viral illness. With proper hydration, rest, and fever control, he would be just fine in a few days. Already starting to prepare discharge instructions for the mother, Cheryl did a final scan of the child's skin, looking for any rashes. When she noticed the red lesion on the child's trunk, she marveled at how closely it resembled all of the pictures in medical textbooks: a dewdrop on a rose petal, the classic presentation of early chickenpox.

For the otherwise healthy toddler and his mother, the virus would be annoying but not dangerous. For Cheryl, it was a potential crisis. She'd never contracted chickenpox as a child; if she became infected, she would be a serious threat to the young cancer patients she was scheduled to care for in her next hospital rotation.

Cheryl wrote discharge instructions for the toddler and then immediately reported the diagnosis to the chief resident. The resident sent her home for two weeks, saying, "Stay away from this

hospital and catch up on your reading." She nodded, waiting until the hospital doors had slid shut behind her to jerk the stethoscope off her neck and grin.

She was thrilled. No early-morning rounds. No beeper. No sleepless nights on call. She raced home, but she had no intention of catching up on her reading. She just wanted to sleep.

• • •

Over the following days, Cheryl had plenty of time to reflect on her career. When she imagined another forty years of darting between exam rooms, wading through stacks of medical records, and fielding late-night telephone calls from patients, the thought that popped into her head was, *How in the world did I end up here, doing this?*

Anyone could see that Cheryl's career trajectory was not a straight path toward medicine but a meandering route full of detours. Far from disappointing her family, friends, and teachers, she had done well in her science classes as an undergraduate at Harvard—but she'd majored in history. She spent her summers between college not volunteering in hospitals but working for nonprofit organizations. After college she deferred medical school to help research a book on the social, economic, and political progress of African Americans after World War II. And halfway through her medical coursework, she completed a master's degree at the Harvard Kennedy School of Government, studying public policy. After that, she deferred again, postponing pediatric residency to start and run a mobile health unit. Echoing Green had funded Cheryl and a partner to bring basic health-care services to people who couldn't afford or access them, including those in communities of color and immigrant communities in Boston.

Those detours suggested that Cheryl's passion wasn't medicine but social justice. Again and again, she had sought opportunities to learn about transforming society and seized chances to put what she'd learned into action. While her parents had tried to create opportunities in the face of injustice, Cheryl wanted to make the world more just in the first place.

She just didn't have the first idea of how to do it. Medicine seemed like the safer choice, guaranteed to make her parents proud and continue to please the other people invested in her success. To get off that path and onto an uncertain one would mean risking failure, seeming ungrateful, or being viewed as unprofessional, flaky, or a quitter.

Mulling it over, Cheryl wished she could stay in quarantine forever. Lying on her couch, watching TV, and eating macaroni and cheese seemed so much more appealing than deciding what to do.

THOSE DETOURS SUGGESTED THAT CHERYL'S PASSION WASN'T MEDICINE BUT SOCIAL JUSTICE.

MARK
DRIVEN TO COLLAPSE

When he returned to college from Sierra Leone, Mark wanted his classmates to be as fervent about stopping genocide as he was. If only they understood the immediacy of the problem, he believed, they would want to tackle it, too.

The first thing he did was put up a website tracking the violence in Darfur. Managing the site took him several hours a week, and only a trickle of visitors came to the page.

Then, in the spring of his junior year, Mark invited the former head of Rwanda's parliament to speak on campus during national Genocide Awareness Month. Like Sierra Leone, Rwanda had endured years of terrible violence during which one ethnic group had systematically slaughtered another. Rwanda was in the news, and a few movies had depicted the suffering there so vividly that many knew about the country's recent bloody history.

Even so, Mark was surprised by how many people turned out to hear the speaker. Students and professors packed the auditorium. They sat in rapt attention while the former head of parliament described the violence he'd seen in his country, the government's inability to stop it, and the lack of international intervention. When the speech was over, the audience members jumped to their feet and gave the speaker a standing ovation.

Elated, Mark stood in the back of the room in his jacket and tie, watching as the audience members nodded and turned to one another. He expected them to discuss how to help Rwanda rebuild and stop the next genocide. He was prepared to step to the front of the room and lead a conversation about what collective action the campus would take. Instead, his classmates picked up their coats and bags and shuffled out of the building. Mark heard someone ask what was for dinner; another pair made plans for the weekend.

He was crushed. He'd successfully brought an important issue to the public's attention but failed to translate their interest into action. Later that evening, Mark talked with a few friends about how to generate popular support for stopping genocide. It wasn't as if people didn't care about genocide, Mark and his friends agreed—the problem was that no one knew what to do about it. Genocide appeared remote and out of control. Even Mark found the idea of stopping genocide overwhelming. As he knew all too well, ending the Holocaust had required a

world war. It was unclear what a handful of well-meaning twenty-year-olds were going to do to turn the tide against centuries of conflict and violence.

A few days later, Mark and the same friends were eating breakfast in the cafeteria and reading the newspaper. They came across a picture in the paper of half a dozen African Union peacekeepers hunkered over a single bowl of rice. These soldiers, men from different African nations deployed to protect African civilians, didn't have enough money to buy food, let alone the equipment and weapons they needed to do their jobs.

Stunned by the picture and what it symbolized, Mark and his friends dove into researching the byzantine and bureaucratic world of international funding agreements. They were deflated by what they learned: In most cases, peacekeepers had to wait for the international community to allocate money to their cause and then wait longer for the funds to work their way through complicated channels to get to them. As a way around this lengthy procedure, Mark and his friends wondered, *Why not raise the money from ordinary citizens?* They could use Mark's website to solicit donations.

With small contributions from a few thousand people, the peacekeepers could buy the basic supplies they needed to help contain the violence.

Mark and one of his friends ditched class to draft an op-ed piece describing their idea. Full of enthusiasm, they fired it off to the *New York Times,* the *Washington Post*, and the *Boston Globe*. No one took the article. The only editor who even responded suggested that their argument would be more persuasive if it didn't come from college students.

Mark started skipping more classes and spending his afternoons in the library, pitching the idea for a citizen-funded, anti-genocide initiative to anyone he thought might listen. He emailed professors, journalists, and human rights activists. He even tried to contact Colin Powell, then U.S. secretary of state, sending messages to various combinations of Mr. Powell's name in the hopes of guessing at the correct email address. If the secretary or his staff had received the message, they didn't answer.

By the end of the semester, Mark was nearly failing three classes. He'd hardly seen his friends. He rarely slept in his own bed; instead, he fell asleep in a chair in the Civic and Social Justice Center, where he'd been trying to generate more online donations. His body may have been tired, but his heart was on full blast.

During exam week, he stayed awake for three days in a row, alternating between studying, maintaining his website, trying to raise money to fund peacekeepers, and volunteering. On his way to tutoring one day at the local elementary school, he collapsed in the middle of the road. The next thing he knew, the school building was receding in the back window of an ambulance, and his head felt as if it were being squeezed between the jaws of an enormous vise.

A paramedic laid his hand on Mark's shoulder. "Hang in there, buddy," he said. "You can make it."

MARDIE
HOME WITHOUT PATRICK

After earning a bachelor's degree in architecture from Rice University in Texas, Mardie took a community development job in Houston. Known as the Bloody Fifth, the Fifth Ward, where Mardie worked, was the city's lowest-income community. Ninety percent of its residents were African American, and most of the rest were Hispanic. The median income was half what Mardie made—and Mardie was barely making ends meet.

Many of the people who lived in the Fifth Ward wanted a piece of the American Dream, but few could afford it. Mardie's organization helped residents clean up their credit, learn about homeownership, and qualify for a loan. Once the clients had been approved for loans, Mardie would find the right lot, use some of the nonprofit's funding to buy it, and build the house using neighborhood subcontractors.

The position fit with her passion for making houses, but it left her frustrated that she couldn't do more. In college, she'd learned that architects design houses, while developers figure out how to build them. But, a lack of funding prevented nonprofit developers from helping everybody who wanted a house.

At night, Mardie worried so much that she started grinding her teeth and had to get a special mouth guard, the kind dentists give fighter pilots who express their stress only while they sleep. She worried about meeting more clients' demand for housing and about the organization's management and financing. But most of all, Mardie worried about Patrick, the little boy she'd met by the backyard swimming pool and ended up looking after for over a decade.

• • •

While Mardie was away at college, Patrick was diagnosed with a rare neurological disorder called ataxia telangiectasia. It didn't affect his intelligence, love of video games, or shy sense of humor, but it made him unsteady on his feet, easily exhausted, and extremely susceptible to cancer. Soon, Patrick was diagnosed with non-Hodgkin's lymphoma. He bravely endured a year of chemotherapy that appeared to send his cancer into remission, but the doctors said the disease could return at any time. While Mardie was working in the Fifth Ward, it did.

After work, as Mardie drove to the hospital, she looked for signs. If a song that

47

Patrick liked came on the radio, she'd tell herself that it was a signal he was going to be okay. Or if the light turned green before she came to a full stop, she took it as an indication that he'd get better. Deep down, she knew that these little symbols didn't mean anything. But they gave her an illusion of control during a time when she felt she had no power over things that mattered deeply to her.

At the Pediatric Intensive Care Unit, two or three families were usually sitting in the waiting room. Mardie hated being there. She hated the patterned, modular furniture organized in rows, a setup that fostered anonymity and isolation, rather than connection and conversation. She hated the fluorescent lighting that made everything stark. She hated the sterile, antiseptic hospital smell that made her feel as if the patients on the other side of the wall weren't people but a biology experiment. Everything about the place amplified her feelings of fear and powerlessness. As soon as she got there, she wanted to scoop up Patrick and leave.

Instead, she stayed with the other families, exchanging thoughts and prayers. When a nurse called her back, Mardie abandoned the waiting room for the cold, bright hospital hallways. As she passed the patient rooms, she could sometimes hear doctors and medical residents shouting, trying to resuscitate a child or prep one quickly for surgery. In other rooms, all Mardie heard was the beep and whoosh of machines keeping children alive.

Mardie was always surprised by how many of these children were alone. After years of following Patrick's treatment, Mardie had learned that family and friends were especially important—not just for emotional support but as advocates for the patient. Mardie had seen firsthand how a miscommunication or a tired doctor could throw off a whole treatment plan, sometimes with catastrophic results. Without someone on the outside paying close attention, a hospital could be a very dangerous place.

At least Patrick had a lot of people looking out for him. When Mardie pushed aside the curtain, she always saw one of his parents already there, dozing in a stiff, hardback chair, or Patrick's sister, sitting on the edge of his bed with her homework spread out on the sheets.

All of them were there when Patrick died. They sang to drown out the machines and held on to his hands and feet so his last sensation would be that of a human touch. When the beeping stopped, a doctor ushered them out of the room. He explained in medical terms what had just happened and then suggested that everyone go home and rest.

Mardie blinked in astonishment. Nothing made sense. What was a home without Patrick?

EVERYTHING ABOUT THE PLACE AMPLIFIED HER FEELINGS OF FEAR AND POWERLESSNESS.

SOCHEATA
IDENTITY UNKNOWN

Socheata's parents had taught her to work with intensity and drive, and she had taken the lesson to heart. She came into the New York City television news studio with the other young producers at exactly 6 a.m., settled into the office, and dispatched one task after another. By 4:00 p.m., she was more than finished. It amazed her that her colleagues stayed so long and fussed over how much they had to do. Calling it research, Socheata watched *Oprah* to avoid leaving inappropriately early.

While the field of news broadcasting generally fit Socheata's interest in storytelling and language, she wasn't making a particularly unique contribution. She was mainly responsible for running scripts to the talent and to the control room; dozens of other recent college graduates throughout the building did the same thing.

Furthermore, Socheata was on permalance status—she worked full-time but didn't get the benefits or job security of a staffer. Her position reminded her every day that she could be replaced.

Even her company's prestige made her feel vulnerable. Socheata had been one of over a hundred applicants, and she went through seven interviews before getting hired. Like Andrew at the consulting firm, she knew she was lucky to get the job, and she wouldn't have dreamed of turning it down. She also knew that ninety-nine people were in line behind her, waiting to take her position if she slipped up or fell out of favor.

To hold on to her job, she made it a point not to call attention to herself. When she thought it was okay to leave, she put her computer on standby and discreetly gathered her things. She liked the people she worked with but didn't want to advertise the fact that she was leaving, so she usually slipped out without saying goodbye, tiptoeing to the elevators. At the studio, she didn't speak out and she didn't leave a mark. She simply treaded lightly, trying not to make a sound.

● ● ●

Almost two years into the job, Socheata finally took a week off and went home for Christmas. Mrs. Poeuv had said she didn't want anything for the holidays except all her children under her roof. As soon as she'd ushered Socheata into the living room, she had her wish. Socheata's sisters were sitting at the breakfast table, their heads close together as they cut fruit and giggled. Her brother was watching TV from a faded wingback chair, a

baseball cap pulled low over his eyes. In the corner, Socheata's father leaned against the fireplace, his rough hands adjusting the stockings that hung from the mantel. From the kitchen, her nephews hollered and came running to hug her. As Socheata kissed her family one by one, Mrs. Poeuv beamed, her eyes wet and her cheeks as rosy as her Christmas sweater.

Socheata's visit passed quickly and pleasantly. She was surprised when, on Christmas Day, her mother called the immediate family into the bedroom. Socheata's sisters went first. Grimacing, Socheata's brother followed, turning

his baseball cap backward. Socheata followed its bill, dread rising in her throat with every step. She wondered what the meeting was about. Behind her, Socheata's father waited until the children were assembled, then he shut the door.

Mrs. Poeuv was already sitting on the bed. Her face looked pale and soft. The wall behind her was empty except for a snapshot of four people in late middle age. Socheata had never studied the photograph or asked who was in it. She thought one of the couples might have been her grandparents.

51

"Pa and I have something to tell you," Mrs. Poeuv said. She clasped her hands between her knees and took a deep breath. Socheata's sisters and brother kept their eyes on the floor, as if they knew what was coming.

"Pa is not my first husband," Mrs. Poeuv said, looking at Socheata. "I was married to another man, and your brother is his son."

Turning to Socheata's sisters, Mrs. Poeuv said, "These are my sister's children. Pa and I took them when she died." Tears rose in Mrs. Poeuv's eyes, and the tip of her nose turned red.

"We, all of us together, we are a family," she concluded. "But I thought you should know. Everybody's growing up. It's good that you know. Okay?"

Socheata stared at her mother. Questions raced through her mind: *What happened to her mother's first husband? Her mother had a sister? How did she die? When were her own sisters adopted? How had her parents met? Why did her father decide to marry a woman who already had a son?*

She looked around the room. Her sisters' faces suddenly appeared foreign. Her brother's narrow shoulders and long arms, which she'd always attributed to her father, seemed out of place. Even her parents seemed like strangers.

Her mother reached over and stroked her arm. "It's so lucky you didn't have to go through all that," she said. "You're the youngest. You've always had a nice life in America. You're the lucky one."

Behind her, Socheata's father choked back a sob. She turned to hug him, but before she could get her arms around him, he ducked into the bathroom and locked the door. The three children he'd raised as his own immediately followed him, assuring him that everything was all right.

Socheata remained alone in the bedroom, enveloped in silence. Now that she knew the truth, she recognized it as the constant undercurrent of her childhood: a penetrating quiet that ran beneath her mother's jokes, her sisters' giggles, her brother's easygoing laugh, her father's attentive gaze. It was as if their American house had been built above a deep well of sorrow, and all the sounds from below were muffled.

Socheata, who'd already been feeling restless, returned to her job at the television studio profoundly unsettled. She didn't feel lucky. She felt lost. Looking toward the future, she couldn't identify any particular direction she wanted to go in. And now, looking at the past, she didn't recognize any roots that might ground her.

BOLD Qs

WHEN IN YOUR LIFE HAVE YOU
FELT OUT OF WHACK?

_____

_____

_____

IN THOSE OUT OF WHACK PERIODS,
WHAT WAS OUT OF BALANCE? WERE YOU
FOLLOWING YOUR HEART? YOUR HEAD?

_____

_____

_____

_____

_____

_____

CHAPTER 3
HEART AND HEAD SYNCING

Feeling out of whack brought at least one benefit to Andrew, Cheryl, Mark, Mardie, and Socheata: Discomfort made change appealing. Whether consciously or unconsciously, they found a way to recalibrate and sync what they felt strongly about with their talents.

To move closer to a meaningful career, pay attention to your heart—what you care about and what you feel. Too often, we ignore our feelings and tell ourselves that we are being too emotional. I ask that you do just the opposite. Listen to what your heart is telling you.

Try new things and observe how you respond. A strong reaction—to a social issue, an organization, a role, or whatever it may be—indicates that you've found something that resonates with you. That reaction may be one of love, empathy, or even great anger or thirst for justice. The information you will get from paying attention to your heart will be eye-opening, possibly surprising, and most definitely helpful.

Your head is also an important part of the equation. By *head,* I mean what you learn in school, what you learn on the job, and all of your best strategic thinking. This definition encompasses what you believe, what you are good at, and the sum of your offerings – your gifts to give. We often choose careers according to how well they suit our intellectual abilities: *Because I'm good at math and science, I'll be an engineer.* But in the search for a career with impact, your head can't meaningfully function alone; it's got to move in step with your heart.

Syncing your heart and head is a choice. Many changemakers find that once they decide to let their entire selves be part of their work, they generate opportunities to work with purpose—to create a life that feels simply right.

ANDREW
THE HUNGER SEASON

After four years at the management consulting firm, Andrew knew he either had to get out of the business world or become more committed to it.

His mother hinted that she'd like for him to be a math professor, and Andrew realized that teaching would be a way to serve others. But education didn't strike Andrew as exactly the right field for him: Like Mardie, he enjoyed applying what he learned himself, rather than passing on his knowledge to others.

Andrew also knew he was well-positioned to advance in business. At the consulting firm, he worked increasingly with senior executives and managed a team of analysts. He had learned how to market products effectively and to think in terms of vast scale. Many of Andrew's clients employed tens of thousands of people and opened new franchises regularly. Andrew was impressed with how powerful and influential corporations could be, and he was steadily acquiring knowledge of how these corporations worked.

It was Andrew's boss who suggested that he could apply what he knew about business to helping those in need. Far from forcing Andrew to forgo his passion, his boss suggested that Andrew lean into it—but to do it strategically and in a way that would get results.

The conversation gave Andrew the encouragement he needed to apply to business school. He reasoned that in business school he could learn how to make the big impact he wanted. He would study how to approach service as a business, demanding metrics, scale, and results. Andrew decided that he could help people most effectively not as a volunteer, but as a CEO.

• • •

In the summer after his first year at Northwestern University's Kellogg Graduate School of Management, when he was twenty-seven, Andrew went on a work-study trip to Africa. He'd never been there before, but he knew that many people on the continent were suffering from illness and poverty. He intended to listen to and learn from the people he wanted to serve, trying to understand where he could best be of use.

As he traveled by bus across the Kenyan countryside, Andrew marveled at the landscape. The wide, blue sky was warm and welcoming. In the distance, a

Because my friends are going hungry

wdydwyd?

These portraits reveal the answer to the question: Why do you do what you do?

jagged mountain ridge rose dramatically. Children played alongside the dusty road, kicking empty Coca-Cola bottles. As they saw Andrew's face in the bus window, they pointed and waved. Andrew waved back. The people he saw seemed friendly and warm.

One woman told him that she'd waited by the side of the road for twenty-four hours with a broken leg while her family collected money to send her to a hospital. Another delivered her own baby, cut the umbilical cord, and returned to work the next day. Andrew was impressed with their stories and touched by how kind, courageous, and diligent they were in the face of desperate poverty.

Eventually, Andrew arrived in Bungoma, Kenya, and met up with a man named Reuben—a contact of a business school friend. Reuben showed Andrew around. The land, parceled into one-acre plots, had been farmed nearly to death. Reuben said that the average Bungoman reaped only half a ton of maize per acre, four times less than a family needed to live. For several months every year, before the new crop was harvested and after the previous year's had been depleted, most people did not have enough to eat. Men, women, children—everybody hovered on the brink of starvation. They called it the hunger season.

Andrew couldn't get his mind around it. With its warm sunshine and gentle rain, Bungoma should have been the most fertile place in the world—and almost everyone there was a farmer. He didn't understand how they couldn't amass enough food to get through an entire year. What was more astonishing was the way people spoke of starvation as a regular part of their lives. Everyone mentioned the hunger season as noteworthy but predictable, like a summer storm. Andrew felt they'd lived in poverty for so long that they simply accepted it.

A few days into his stay, Andrew met Christine, a widow who lived with her children in a mud hut surrounded by an acre of thin brown maize. It was midsummer, and the crops were already withering.

Christine invited Andrew inside while she prepared the day's only meal. Her children waited patiently, their eyes big and their bellies swollen with worms. One of Christine's five children had already died several years ago; another was very sick, but Christine couldn't afford to take her to the hospital. In the dim light, Andrew watched Christine stir flour into tin cups of hot water and hand one to each of her children. They slurped up the thin paste. One of the boys looked up at Andrew. His mouth was rimmed with white.

Andrew had to step outside. He took off his glasses and rubbed his eyes. To see children drinking nothing but flour and water was almost more than he could handle. It was unfair, and it made him feel helpless, even worthless. His desire to make a difference in Christine's life—and in the lives of other hungry farmers in Bungoma—was overwhelming. As it had been when he gave the woman in Mexico his last five dollars, Andrew's heart was fully engaged.

But this time, Andrew's head also kicked in. He put his glasses back on and looked around. One of Christine's neighbors had a full, lush garden. His children were playing between stalks of tall green maize. These children looked healthy and well-groomed; their parents could afford to buy them school uniforms, and they were getting an education. The neighbor's thriving farm proved that growing decent crops in Western Kenya was possible. Therefore, Andrew reasoned, the origins of the hunger season weren't agricultural.

He wondered if there might be a way to approach the hunger season from an economic angle. He thought back to what he'd learned in college, as a management consultant, and in business school. He remembered the college professor who taught him how a functioning market worked. Bungoma was not too different from the desert island the professor had described, in which one person had two pairs of pants and the other two shirts. The farmers in Western Kenya didn't need handouts; they had valuable natural resources. What they lacked was a way to trade for what they didn't yet have. The solution was a classic functioning market. Andrew believed he could harness trade, capital, investments, savings, and technology to make the farms in Bungoma produce enough food for the entire year.

Of course, Andrew realized he would have to figure out how to harness the market not only for profit but also for social change. He would have to consider factors businesses didn't always have to take into account: culture, health, and education. Andrew's challenge would be more complex—and have higher stakes—than any of the multibillion-dollar businesses for which he had consulted.

He could hardly wait. Still standing in the bright sun, Andrew mentally christened his idea "One Acre Fund."

BUT THIS TIME, ANDREW'S HEAD ALSO KICKED IN.

CHERYL
PIECES OF A PUZZLE

At the end of her pediatric residency, Cheryl's dread of spending the next forty years in a hospital outweighed the dread of disappointing others and herself. She hated the thought of letting down all the people who had invested in her over the years and who cared deeply about her success. She had become a doctor primarily because of her deep desire to serve. That desire still compelled her, but it didn't change the fact that she didn't actually enjoy the work. So after almost a decade of training, she summoned the courage to announce that she wasn't going to be a practicing physician; she was leaving medicine.

The blow was softened by her moving into another prestigious role. Cheryl won a highly competitive White House Fellowship that exposed her to the highest branches of government. Public policy was much closer to her heart than medicine. The satisfaction that the work gave her was much more important than the satisfaction of the honor bestowed. Yet even as she marveled at top government officials' ability to navigate the political system, she realized that, temperamentally, she wasn't suited for the political back-and-forth.

Acknowledging her bookish nature, she enrolled in graduate school to pursue a Ph.D. program in history. The stories enshrined in the historical texts were more remote than she expected they would be. She missed engaging with the people she was serving. After a year she left school and took a short-lived job with a for-profit company, which underscored what she knew all along: She was simply not motivated by money, and the promise of financial reward was irrelevant if she wasn't enthusiastic about a company's mission.

Eventually Cheryl tried so many things that family and friends made a running joke of asking for her new business card. She knew their teasing only hid their concern, but her professional twists and turns sometimes made Cheryl feel as if her darkest fears had been realized: She was a failure who did not fit in anywhere. Nonetheless, she kept trying new career paths and trusting that she would eventually find the right one. During these years, Cheryl was finally learning to recognize and heed the messages her heart *and* head were sending her.

● ● ●

Because I Heard the Universe Whisper my path and heeded its call.

wdydwyd?

Cheryl's work experience may not have proceeded in a straight line, but it had value to her. Practicing medicine taught her both what it meant to be of service in helping others and how to use information effectively. Practicing public policy at the Harvard Kennedy School and through the White House Fellows program gave her an understanding of how various actors advocate for their point of view to bring about change. And her academic work over the years had shown her example after example of how individuals and communities struggle to build meaningful lives for themselves,

occasionally sacrificing everything for justice and opportunity.

At thirty-eight, in the midst of some consulting gigs, Cheryl was asked to take over as the head of Echoing Green, where she was a board member. Echoing Green had long been an important organization in Cheryl's life. It had invested in her when she was in medical school, funding her and a partner to start a mobile health center. The years Cheryl spent running the Family Van were among the happiest of her professional life. On those days she ran the Family Van, Cheryl walked from the hallowed halls of Harvard

Medical School, across the trolley tracks on Huntington Avenue, and into the Mission Hill neighborhood. The distance was less than one city block, but the two places might as well have been on different planets. Cheryl felt equally at home in both. She could communicate with elite, pedigreed doctors, professors, and policymakers as easily as she could with disadvantaged community residents, street-smart adolescents, and tired, struggling adults. They were all familiar to her—variations on her neighbors growing up, her extended family, her parents, or her classmates and colleagues. She had always assumed that her inability to fit neatly into one category was a detriment. Working with the Family Van, she had a revelation: Her mutability was actually an asset. Being "the other" was a strength, one that ultimately allowed her to fit in *everywhere*. She wouldn't fully leverage that strength again until she ran Echoing Green.

As president of a nonprofit that funds social entrepreneurs, Cheryl's responsibility was to move among a variety of groups, translating their needs to one another. She connected the applicants with the donors, the staff with the board, and the people who were being advocated for with the people who made policy—over and over speaking up for those couldn't speak for themselves. Cheryl's heart had always been drawn to service; once she found that her unique qualities were a gift, and not a burden, she was able to sync her heart with her head and begin helping people with great energy and success.

BEING "THE OTHER" WAS A STRENGTH, ONE THAT ULTIMATELY ALLOWED HER TO FIT IN EVERYWHERE.

MARK
UPPING THE ANTE

Mark woke up in the hospital. After three days without sleep, he'd had a grand mal seizure. The doctors determined he wasn't suffering from epilepsy or any other medical condition. He was simply exhausted. When Mark was released, he was too weak and tired to work on the anti-genocide campaign, let alone study.

The seizure was a wakeup call. Mark realized he needed to use his time and energy more effectively. While Cheryl had to learn to listen to her heart, Mark realized that he needed to bring his head into the equation—if he wanted to achieve his goal of stopping genocide, he'd have to be strategic as well as passionate. To align his heart and head, he took a step back and reassessed what he was doing.

He made an important first step, one all changemakers take: He did the research. After he'd recovered from the seizure and scheduled makeup exams for his classes, Mark found out every-thing he could about genocide. He talked to his professors, he read books and articles, and he interviewed experts. Understanding the history of his issue and what had already been done to address it gave Mark not only perspective but credibility. To propose his own ideas about social change, he needed to show

that he knew what he was talking about.

In his research, the most important thing Mark learned was that genocide is not inevitable. It is not a phenomenon or a natural disaster. People choose to begin genocides, which meant people can also choose to stop them.

The idea of making deliberate choices to help other people resonated with Mark. His home had taught him to have great faith in and respect for people. After all, his grandparents escaped the Holocaust because strangers had given them refuge. He had also seen how many ordinary citizens contributed money to African Union peacekeepers. In the few months since he and several of his friends had started accepting donations on their website, traffic had surged, and they had raised $250,000.

But Mark also realized that collecting donations from individual citizens wasn't enough. The more he read about geno-cide, the more he saw stopping it as a kind of chess game. He came to know who the players were, what moves they could make, and how their opponents might win. And he saw that nearly every win-ning move involved the government. Bills, mandates, policies, and legislation: These were the tools to solve Mark's problem,

just as Andrew's tools were trade, capital, investment, savings, and technology. If Mark wanted to stop genocide, he'd have to get political.

On a cool day in the spring of their senior year in college, Mark and a friend put on suits and took a bus from Swarthmore, Pennsylvania, to Washington, D.C. They were twenty-one years old and didn't know anything about lobbying Congress—Mark's last real experience with the government was watching "I'm Just a Bill" on *Schoolhouse Rock*. They weren't even entirely sure how to find the Capitol building.

Fortunately, from the bus station they saw its white dome reaching high into the sky, and they followed its silhouette right to the front door.

On their initial visit, Mark and his friend went to several congressional offices. They didn't speak to the representatives directly—visitors rarely do—but they sat down with staffers and explained the violence unfolding in Darfur. They asked for the United States to allocate more funding to stop it and to impose diplomatic and economic sanctions.

The staffers couldn't promise anything, but Mark was impressed by how polite and interested they were. He was also struck by how little some of them seemed to know about the issue. They *welcomed* the information he provided. The visit reinforced Mark's commitment to researching his issue. It also gave him strong evidence that people respond best when asked to do something concrete. He noticed that if he spoke about genocide in general terms, the staffers grew restless, but if he asked them to persuade their Congress member to vote one way or the other, they nodded and jotted down a note.

Too many activists simply rallied for their cause, Mark noted; he intended to approach the people who had the power to help him and to solicit their support with respect and clear objectives. He decided to ask for what he wanted just as his mother's effective customers had asked for what they wanted when they arrived at her airline counter.

While Mark's visit to D.C. taught him a lot, several months later, he and his friend didn't see any tangible results from their trip. The violence in Darfur continued, and Congress hadn't intervened. Mark persisted in his efforts. He continued to build his knowledge about the conflict and to update the website. Money and visitors kept slowly coming.

One afternoon, a woman he didn't know tracked him down through his website and said she'd like to donate some money—not to the peacekeepers but to Mark's movement. Mark had never thought of his efforts as a movement. He believed he was doing a community service project with a couple of friends. But once the woman pointed out that he had an entire army of people reading his website and contributing money, Mark could see there was more momentum behind him than he'd realized.

Shyly, Mark asked his benefactor for some cash to buy pizza and soda for anyone willing to go to D.C. and lobby Congress with him. She upped the ante: She'd donate $100 for every person Mark and his friend could get to go to D.C.

The offer made Mark nervous. It seemed rude to discuss money and was embarrassing to admit that he needed it. Nevertheless, he recognized the generosity of the woman's offer and agreed to accept her donation of $100 a head.

Three weeks later, Mark and his classmates ushered 100 people into the largest hearing room in the Senate. After a few minutes, one of the Pennsylvania senators emerged and listened to their request. It was possible that he was already interested in stopping genocide, but it certainly didn't hurt that prospective voters were making the case for action in Darfur. Moreover, they'd given up a day to visit him, and all had donated to the cause. Votes, time, and money had weight in Washington, and Mark could see that the senator was impressed. As Mark stood in the back of the room, listening to his classmates put their voices behind their dollars, he felt he'd come a long way since failing to capitalize on the speech given by the head of the Rwandan parliament. He had finally learned how to translate the public's interest in genocide into action. His heart and head finally synced.

A week later, Mark received a check in the mail, along with a note from his benefactor asking what else she could do. This time, he didn't hesitate. He realized that she was helping not him but a cause to which she was deeply committed. Stopping genocide was a bold, ambitious goal that required bold, ambitious action. It would require hundreds of thousands, if not millions, of ordinary citizens, a significant online presence, a media campaign, and extensive political organizing. He couldn't stop genocide on his own, but he could do it with a strategic network of passionate supporters.

With three friends, Mark drew up a plan for an advocacy organization called the Genocide Intervention Network. He sent it to his benefactor, along with a request for $2 million.

STOPPING GENOCIDE WAS A BOLD, AMBITIOUS GOAL THAT REQUIRED BOLD, AMBITIOUS ACTION.

MARDIE
THE SWEET SPOT

After Patrick died, Mardie woke up in the mornings sick to her stomach. Her grief felt like a fist—a hard, clenched knot that she expected to stay in her forever. The sadness made her want to stay in bed. Nevertheless, she had set a plan into motion before Patrick's last diagnosis, and in part to distract herself from the pain, she forced herself to continue what she'd begun.

Mardie left her job with the community development organization in the Fifth Ward and studied finance, earning her MBA. At thirty-three, she took a position as a lender in Northern California. Just like Mardie's previous employer, this organization invested in affordable housing projects; this time, however, Mardie was on the other side of the table. Instead of asking for money, she was investing $34 million in debt capital from banks, the government, and a very wealthy philanthropist.

The role was uncomfortable for her. She still considered herself a creative type, and her educator parents regarded the business world with suspicion. But Mardie's job in the Fifth Ward had taught her that a developer builds only what she can finance, and if she wanted to create houses for people who needed them, she had to learn how to get the money. She began to picture her career as a Venn diagram: Architecture was one circle, community development another, and financing a third. Time, learning, and opportunity allowed her to keep adding circles to her diagram, and she had faith that one day they would finally all come together in the middle.

* * *

One of Mardie's clients was a group of advocates working on behalf of residents at Agnews Developmental Center. The Center opened its doors in 1888 as one of California's first institutions for the care and treatment of the mentally ill, housing as many as 4,500 people at a time. When first constructed, it was surrounded by orchards; over time, the surrounding area changed dramatically, and the institution was now located in the heart of the tech industry in Silicon Valley.

One afternoon, Mardie toured the eighty-acre campus. She could see why it was slated for closure. The facility was old and in disrepair, and its one-size-fits-all caregiving model needed an overhaul, too. Patients slept three and four to a room. Instead of closets, they each had a freestanding wardrobe in which to

store their few belongings. They shared bathrooms. The cafeteria had been so thoroughly used that Mardie could no longer distinguish single smells—it was just a vague, suffocating blend of odors.

Many of the patients had been in the institution for decades, and they didn't seem to be making progress. Mardie was shown the recreation room, which was located in the building reserved for the most medically fragile residents. It was a hot summer day, and because the airconditioning wasn't working, the windows were open. The twelve patients in the room had between them cerebral palsy, brain damage, and epilepsy. All were in a wheelchair or gurney, and all required special equipment—a feeding tube or an IV drip. While all of the patients had been set up to face the TV, the positioning of their equipment meant that none of them could actually see the screen. Instead, they gazed at the ceiling or at a wall, their eyes vacant and unblinking beneath fluorescent lights.

With a shudder, Mardie remembered the Pediatric Intensive Care Unit where she'd visited Patrick. Even though Agnews' staff was caring and generous, the building had the impersonal, sterile feel of a hospital. Nothing seemed designed for comfort or health; instead, the decor and layout of the rooms made it impossible for patients to get a good night's sleep and ensured that visitors would dread walking in the door.

By the time Mardie toured the campus, Agnews had been in the process of closing for almost ten years. The building might have been uncomfortable, but it was home to the patients, and it was unclear where they would go once the facility closed. Moving residents out of an institution was an incredibly complex undertaking that involved a dizzying number of stakeholders and required bringing together creative financing resources, ownership structures, and service models. The more Mardie discussed it with Agnews' staff, advocates, caregivers, financers, and families, the more it occurred to her that she was in the unique position to understand all the variables. Her architecture degree taught her design; her work in the Fifth Ward exposed her to development, construction, and creating community; and her work as a lender made her fluent in financing. Mardie could envision a future where each resident of Agnews could live in a home designed to accommodate his or her individual needs. The houses would be beautiful, welcoming, and comfortable—spaces that nurtured their bodies, and that encouraged family and friends to visit.

In creating an alternative to Agnews, Mardie found the sweet spot where the circles in her Venn diagram overlapped. There was a fourth circle, too, she realized: Patrick. He had taught her that special needs don't preclude joy. In the right surroundings, people with special needs could be relaxed, comfortable, and supported in homes of their own. As Mardie fully imagined this new organization, Hallmark Community Solutions, a great joy filled her chest. It was so big that it even loosened the grip that grief had on her.

SOCHEATA
NEW YEAR BABY

Six months after her mother's shocking announcement, Socheata took advantage of a break between contracts at the television studio and went to Cambodia with her parents and brother. It seemed to be a good chance to learn about her family and to also put her journalism skills to use in a very personal way. Before she left, she borrowed a film camera from the studio and asked a friend to teach her how to use it. For her first lesson, he taught her how to turn it on.

The camera turned out to be an unwelcomed addition to the trip. Socheata's parents were happy for her to film the local sites, but they refused to be interviewed, and her aunts and uncles also turned away from the camera's lens. Socheata found that the people she met in Cambodia, like her family members, did not want to talk about the past.

Most of what she knew about the country's recent history came from books. She knew that the Khmer Rouge government had intended to erase the class divisions between people of Chinese ancestry and the peasants who worked the fields. They seized citizens' property and homes, killing many in the process, and marched them into labor camps. The citizens slept together in

flimsy dwellings, quickly getting sick and spreading illnesses. During the day they maintained farms, growing rice and grain. Guards watched them all the time. To keep the citizens from fomenting a rebellion, the Khmer Rouge kept them on the verge of starvation. If they fell ill, they didn't get real medicine but instead placebos.

Every Cambodian was affected. Approximately one quarter of the population died during the Khmer Rouge regime. Some groups, like ethnic Chinese, suffered heavier losses. About half of Socheata's extended family on her mother's side died.

Yet, in Socheata's experience, it was as if the Khmer Rouge genocide had never happened. She'd never learned about it in school, even though it had occurred during many of her teachers' lifetimes. And in Phnom Penh, the capital of Cambodia, she saw mostly people her own age trying to move into the future: young men driving motorbikes, young women traipsing in and out of internet cafés.

Socheata filmed the blur of traffic and shops from the backseat of the rental car. At one point, her mother said, "There's my old apartment," and pointed to a

to make my parents' sacrifice worth it

wdydwyd?

second-story window above a brightly lit boutique. "I lived there with my first husband, before you were born," she told Socheata's brother. He twisted his head to look, and Socheata swung her camera and zoomed on the window—but the curtain was drawn, and whatever was behind it remained obscure. The past appeared permanently hidden behind grief, fear, and silence.

• • •

In their final week in Cambodia, Socheata talked her father into taking her to the labor camp where he and her mother had

worked. She expected to see the remains of the camp, evidence of some farms, perhaps a cemetery. Instead, her father stopped the car at an empty field. Thick bright grass covered any trace of what had once grown beneath it.

Without speaking, Socheata's father walked to the field. She trailed after him with the video camera, not expecting to get any good footage. There was nothing to see here, she thought. It seemed to be the story of her entire trip.

She followed her father past some saplings. He walked directly to a concrete block that jutted out from the soft soil.

"This was the latrine," her father said softly. "We buried your aunt near here after she died."

Looking at that concrete artifact, Socheata felt bad that her aunt had been left in such an undignified place. But for her father, the presence of a relative's body made this hallowed ground. He raised his hands to his face and sobbed.

Tears welled in Socheata's own eyes. Of course, she thought: Her parents knew that the concrete building, unlike the bamboo structures and the fields, would last. They had buried her aunt here so they could find her body again. They must have planned to come back later and have a proper service.

Socheata put her arms around her father's shoulders and laid her forehead against his neck. Listening to him cry gave her a new perspective on the silence that seemed to penetrate her parents' generation. Perhaps survivors *wanted* to remember, she thought. They *wanted* to talk about what happened. It was just hard to do, and they didn't have a way.

Socheata vowed that if her parents wanted to tell their story, she'd be there to hear what they had to say.

• • •

It was Socheata's mother who broke the silence. On the drive back to the airport, she described seeing Socheata's father in the labor camp for the first time. He was thin and lanky, and his skin was dark from years of working in the fields. She didn't like him. She herself came from a well-off, Chinese-born family, and when she passed Mr. Poeuv, she shot him dirty looks. He didn't particularly like her, either, but he noticed she was taking care of a young son and two nieces. He saw that her heart was kind.

The guards at the labor camp noticed Socheata's parents, too. Since the Khmer Rouge wanted to equalize the society, the regime looked for opportunities to put together people from different social classes. Socheata's parents fit the bill. They came from different worlds, and they both needed partners; her father was single, and her mother was widowed. One night, officials came to Mr. Poeuv's room and announced that all the bachelors were going to be married. There was no choice. The Poeuvs' union began at the end of a gun.

Socheata captured her mother's narration on tape. A year later, she returned to Cambodia to explore the rest of her parents' journey, including their escape to a refugee camp in Thailand, where she'd been born on New Year's Day. She told the story of how her father had stolen across the border three times, in the middle of the night, to bring in each of the other children. At the end of the film, Socheata taped an anniversary party she threw for her parents. She wanted to honor the fact that they'd stayed together, forged a family, and kept alive the dedication, loyalty, and love that the Khmer Rouge regime had threatened to wipe out.

In making the film, Socheata had to confront feelings that her family had tried to protect her from and to ask her parents to speak frankly about subjects they'd avoided. Using her skills as a journalist and the strength she found by tapping into her heart, she pushed through some of her own discomfort to do justice to her parents' and Cambodia's history. The Khmer Rouge regime had destroyed part of its own population and scarred the rest. Socheata wanted to speak out against their actions, while trying to uncover how such a thing could happen. She found that her task wasn't that of an amateur filmmaker or a journalist but that of a storyteller.

Her family's story, *New Year Baby*, aired on national television. It was the first film by a Cambodian American to explore the Khmer Rouge regime. At twenty-seven, Socheata earned the iWitness Human Rights Award.

After making the film and receiving the award, she assumed that her job was done. It wasn't.

PERHAPS SURVIVORS WANTED TO REMEMBER, SHE THOUGHT. THEY WANTED TO TALK ABOUT WHAT HAPPENED.

BOLD Qs

WHAT WOULD YOU DO IF YOU WERE NOT AFRAID OF FAILING?

_____

_____

_____

_____

WHAT CAN YOU DO THAT DRAWS ON BOTH YOUR HEART AND YOUR HEAD?

_____

_____

_____

_____

_____

_____

WHY DO YOU DO WHAT YOU DO?

_____

_____

_____

_____

_____

_____

wdydwyd?

The project has challenged over one
million people to answer: "Why do you do
what you do?" Upload your answer or sign
up to collaborate at www.wdydwyd.com.

CHAPTER 4
HUSTLE

If you've synced your heart and head as you make career choices, hustle is not far behind. Hustle is a state of being "in the zone"–impact-driven and heading toward change.

Hustle mode looks different for everyone. For some, it is about thinking bigger than they ever could have imagined; for others, it is about feeling more energy to do more–again, more than they thought possible. Hustle mode means the ability to be effective, driven by results, and satisfied, because you are doing what you are supposed to do. You are on an informed path that you have chosen. You are working with purpose.

This is not to say changemakers never experience bad days, disappointments, or setbacks. Sometimes their lives again fall out of whack. But they use the tools of reflection and self-awareness to bring their hearts and heads back into sync. When an opportunity arises for the two to click, they make the bold choice to commit and see the work through.

In many ways, the process is cyclical: Syncing your heart and head produces hustle, which produces impact, which produces more personal happiness, which produces more impact—and the momentum helps carry you forward.

Andrew, Mark, Cheryl, Mardie, and Socheata entered into hustle mode when they struck the right balance between commitment to their work and attention to themselves and their personal relationships. Choosing a path required them each to push through resistance—personal, professional, and societal. But once they were fully invested, these changemakers found a clarity of purpose and the perseverance to carry the work through. Because they were in hustle mode, they were able to overcome many of the obstacles that had first seemed daunting, and to work on purpose: achieving significant social impact in an area about which they were passionate, applying the gifts they were given and the skills they had learned.

ANDREW
APPETITE FOR GROWTH

Andrew returned to Bungoma to find his new employees sitting on plastic chairs in an empty office, leafing through paperwork. They weren't entirely sure what they were supposed to do.

Andrew wasn't sure, either. He was fresh out of business school. He hadn't even picked up his diploma; he'd just taken his final exam and caught the first plane to Kenya. When he looked at his staff's expectant faces and glanced out the window at the barren fields, all he could think was that he'd made a terrible mistake.

He pushed through his doubts because he was deeply invested in helping hungry farmers feed themselves. His idea was to combine all the services they needed and make sure all the elements worked together in a functioning economy. His team loaned a small group of farmers some money to get started, distributed better seeds and fertilizer, and hired local Kenyans to teach the farmers how to use these materials effectively. In the first year, the farmers increased their yield fourfold. They had enough to eat, as well as leftover grain to sell.

One Acre Fund bought the leftover grain, sold it, and reinvested the revenues in the organization to help pay for an additional set of farmers to learn the process. By its second year, One Acre Fund had quintupled in size, and by its fifth year, it served more than 30,000 farm families and employed more than 450 staff members.

● ● ●

Andrew's drive to succeed has motivated him to set big goals. As a consultant, he worked with companies that brought in a minimum of $4 billion in revenue every year; some were earning over $30 billion. They had international franchises and 10,000-person staffs. As a businessman working on behalf of the poor, Andrew is growing the One Acre Fund to operate at the scale of a large corporation. *Why should we serve only those farmers from Bungoma or Kenya or even East Africa?* he asks. *Why not all of Africa? Why not south and Southeast Asia? Why not the world?*

Andrew's appetite for growth is voracious. If his plans succeed, he will make a significant dent for the 500 million people who live on subsistence farms worldwide.

● ● ●

On an ordinary day, Andrew wakes when the fat African sun has just peeked above

the horizon. He climbs out of bed rested and refreshed, stirs some instant coffee into a mug of water, and, in shorts and T-shirt, pads barefoot across the concrete floor and turns on his laptop.

Many of Andrew's tasks resemble those he performed for the consulting firm. He scans a price list, looking for a better deal on seeds and fertilizer. Because so many of his clients live in rural, remote areas, transporting supplies to each of them is expensive. If Andrew finds a company that will deliver seeds and fertilizer in bulk, he calls and asks if they are willing to drive a little farther in

exchange for more clients.

It's a routine business calculation, no different from haggling with an airline supplier. But Andrew is delighted to do it because he is negotiating on behalf of poor farmers, and he knows that every penny he saves helps someone climb out of poverty.

In the afternoon, Andrew visits his clients' farms. Reuben, the first person he met in Bugoma, walks with him to the end of the road. They practice Swahili. To quiz Andrew on his vocabulary, Reuben points to the tin roofs that many farmers have added to their houses, to

in the crops before they'd reached their peak. Now, Andrew sees little evidence of hunger. Families still have last year's grain in their storehouses, and they can afford to let the fields grow a final few inches and ripen in the sun.

With the sun at its highest point in the afternoon sky, Andrew pulls over to check on one of his newest clients. Before he knocks on her door, he steps into her plot of land, reaches above his head, and pulls down one of the stalks. He comes face-to-face with an ear of maize as long and thick as his forearm. It is a meal in itself.

As Andrew looks at the maize, it seems magical to him that the food simply grew. A rich person didn't have to give it to a poor person, and a poor person didn't have to wait for it helplessly. Andrew's client could, by her own efforts, meet her needs and replenish her supplies every year. That he could witness such a miracle strikes Andrew as a privilege. As a teenager, Andrew was happy to be able to hand over his last five dollars to a hungry woman and child; now, he marvels that his work sustains many men, women, and children. He never imagined that he would end up in the middle of a farm in Africa, running a $10 million nonprofit organization to help the poor feed themselves, but now that he is here, he takes off his glasses and smiles up at the sky.

children whose parents can now afford to buy them uniforms and send them to school, and to a woman carrying a book. Evidence of One Acre Fund's success is everywhere, and Andrew names all of it.

Seeing how he's improved the lives of the people around him helps Andrew cope with the occasional bout of homesickness. Besides, almost all the farmers he met on his initial visit, including Christine, have become not only clients but friends. As his car passes their one-acre plots, Andrew waves to familiar faces among the tall, sturdy stalks of maize. The harvest is only a week away. Before, these days just before the harvest marked the worst of the hunger season, when families had been starving for months and trying to resist bringing

CHERYL
SHOUTING OUT LOUD

Cheryl sang softly under her breath and tapped her foot to the beat. She related to the singer's lyrics: "'Cause everybody's got a part in the game....And everybody's got a cross they can claim....And everybody's got somebody to blame....But we all must find our own way, yeah, yeah." By the time the chorus rolled around, she just couldn't help herself. As if she were a back-up singer, Cheryl belted out the refrain—"I wanna shout out, shout out loud"—not caring one bit if she embarrassed herself.

It was the evening of the third Be Bold Awards, Echoing Green's annual tribute to changemakers from the world of social entrepreneurship, business, and the arts. Amos Lee, Cheryl's favorite singer, was finishing up his last song after receiving a Be Bold Award for his work supporting arts programs for kids in his native Philadelphia.

More than 500 people were assembled in the opulent, 4,800-square-foot ballroom in the historic Prince George. Built in 1904, the residence was once one of New York City's premier hotels; after many years of decline, it was rehabilitated by Common Ground, a pioneer in the development of supportive housing, and reopened in 1999. Just beyond the

ballroom's entrance, the real work of the Prince George occurred: providing permanent, affordable housing for over 400 low-income and formerly homeless people living with HIV/AIDS.

As a DJ took over, mixing neo-soul with house music, and the guests talked and laughed, Cheryl looked around truly happy. She recognized Echoing Green alumni mingling with newly selected Echoing Green Fellows. The Social Investment Council, a group of socially conscious young professionals in for-profit fields like law, finance, consulting, and marketing, danced alongside nonprofit leaders and hedge fund managers. Together, the guests contributed financial, mentoring, networking, and technical advisory services to Echoing Green.

As she took it all in, Cheryl posed the same question she had asked herself as a medical resident many years before: *How in the world did I end up here, doing this?* But this time, she knew exactly why she was there, who she was, and what she was doing.

Cheryl believes with every fiber of her being that individuals can change the world. Some do it through the social sector, while others do it through

business and government. She also believes that while everyone has a different approach, people in all industries succeed because they are passionate about a cause for which their unique skills and talents are ideally suited. And they work on their issue smarter, harder, and better than almost anyone else.

Cheryl, too, is a changemaker. Her sphere of concern is the social sector, where people like the Echoing Green Fellows attempt to solve the problems confronting their communities. For many, it will be their life's work, requiring legions of champions and supporters.

This is the work of social movements—collective action and mobilization of resources—that yields significant change. They build solutions to today's problems for a better, more just tomorrow.

The lights of the ballroom flickered, signaling that it was time for the festivities to end. Cheryl made her final rounds among the guests, trying to touch base with a number of current Echoing Green Fellows before they left for the evening. She was eager to hear updates or schedule follow-ups to discuss any concerns or problems. She also had Echoing Green board members to thank—leaders who care deeply about championing and supporting the next generation—and a staff to manage and support. As Cheryl moved through the crowd, chatting with partygoers of diverse races, classes, ages, and ideologies, she embodied the alignment of passion and skill in service of the cause that inspired her most: building solutions to today's problems for a more promising future. She thought how lucky she was to have her job. But by "lucky" she didn't mean that she had stumbled into her role by chance. An adherent of the wisdom of leaders as ancient as Seneca and as modern as Oprah, Cheryl believes that luck is the meeting of preparation and opportunity. The lucky moments are those that lead you to where you belong.

HOW IN THE WORLD DID I END UP HERE, DOING THIS?

MARK
B+ TO A

Mark and some friends started the Genocide Intervention Network (GI-NET) in 2005, the summer after they graduated from college. He was working too hard to notice whether he was in hustle mode. He arrived at his Washington, D.C. office at 8:30 a.m. each morning and left in the middle of the night.

He carried out almost everything in the organization's strategic plan. He called donors, traveled to colleges and universities to speak to students about genocide, kept track of new books and articles on the topic, and followed foreign policy legislation in Congress.

There was all the organizational stuff, too. Along with his three colleagues, Mark coded the website, scrubbed the database, hammered out press releases, wrote grants, and kept track of the accounting. When GI-NET received a little more money, Mark interviewed candidates and hired more staff. His new employees took over some of the work, but he still had to figure out how to manage the staff's time, arrange for their paychecks and health insurance, and acquire desks and computers for everybody.

GI-NET still used the easy online donation strategy that Mark had created in college, through which anybody could chip in to pay for African Union peacekeepers. The site now included all sorts of ways for users to take political action. After all, governments have the ultimate power to stop genocide. GI-NET made it easy for anybody interested in ending genocide to hold their representatives accountable. Visitors to GI-NET's site could find out who their congressional representatives were and email them asking them to help end genocide. They could dial an 800 number and talk to someone in their representative's office. They could sign a petition. They could even track legislation in Congress that would help stop genocide. To hold legislators accountable, GI-NET issued report cards for members of Congress, giving each a grade for his or her performance on stopping genocide.

Mark and his colleagues had found an advocacy strategy that worked. They were able to pass legislation, conduct field work overseas, make genocide a topic in political campaigns, and generate publicity in the media.

Their success meant that they had more opportunities to make an impact. But GI-NET couldn't keep growing into its potential if Mark and his colleagues continued their pattern of trying to

do everything at once. They needed to figure out how to be more strategic. On a summer day two years after GI-NET's founding, Mark took a step back and reconsidered where he could make the biggest difference in the organization.

His heart was certainly not in the day-to-day details of the operation. When he sat down to choose health insurance or organize paychecks, he quickly became bored. To procrastinate, he picked up the phone and talked to a potential donor or sent an email to someone who had invited him to speak. By not tackling mundane tasks immediately, Mark let them drag on

hours longer than they should have. He concluded that if he didn't enjoy doing something, he probably wasn't very good at it, and he should pass on the responsibility to someone who was.

He also noticed that whenever a new opportunity came along, one of his co-founders' attention immediately turned to legislation: *What bills were in committee? What should the policy say?* In contrast, Mark thought first of people. *Who do we know who can help us?* he wondered. *What congressperson should we talk to?* Mark's address book contained thousands of entries. His acquaintances

89

and his colleagues reimagined the organization. Mark would pull back from the policy work and the day-to-day operations. Instead, he'd focus on giving speeches, visiting schools, and raising money. He would put his best skills into the service of his dearest passion—and as a result, provide the people-fuel GI-NET needed to move ahead.

The decision filled Mark with energy. He imagined all the time he'd have in the upcoming weeks and months to speak to the people who could help his organization the most. In his mind's eye, he pictured a handful of students he thought could drum up a crowd of 10,000 people, a businessman who'd hinted he might make an investment, and an early supporter of GI-NET who now had a position in the White House. Each of these people had the potential to make a real impact, and he couldn't wait to start making phone calls and setting up appointments.

• • •

One afternoon not long after the staff retreat, the cell phone on Mark's desk rang. He picked it up on the first half-ring, not even looking at the caller ID. His eyes were glued to the computer: a Jewish representative from Ohio had just been named to the Foreign Relations Committee, and Mark was using Google

weren't just people he'd met superficially—he'd talked to them, found out what they knew, and turned them into stakeholders.

Just as Andrew thought in terms of numbers, and Socheata in terms of stories, Mark thought in terms of relationships and social networks. He recognized that for his organization to grow, he needed to tap into one of the skills he'd learned from his parents: talking to people.

At a staff retreat by the Washington Monument on the National Mall, Mark

Earth to find out where all the synagogues in Cleveland were. He figured the congregations would want to know how energetically their representative was working to stop genocide, and he intended to encourage them to make their voices heard.

Mark was so busy thinking about the impact of the voices of hundreds of Jewish men and women demanding an end to genocide that he jumped when he heard the voice on the other end of the phone. It was a congresswoman asking to speak to Mr. Hanis.

She was polite but direct. She said she'd learned she had earned only a B+ on GI-NET's anti-genocide report card. How could she get an A?

Mark broke into a grin. He knew GI-NET had just entered a new phase. Politicians were feeling pressure from their constituents, and they were willing to do something to stop genocide. Without missing a beat, Mark described the legislation coming up in Congress and told her what GI-NET recommended she do. He had figured out how to deploy his talents by syncing his heart and head. He had entered into hustle mode, and the effect would be life-changing for him and for the victims of genocide.

HE HAD FIGURED OUT HOW TO DEPLOY HIS TALENTS BY SYNCING HIS HEART AND HEAD.

MARDIE
WIDENING CIRCLES

Mardie's hustle comes in the form of being able to take on enormous challenges—not with stress and anxiety, but with humor and grace.

Her organization, now called Hello Housing (formerly Hallmark Community Solutions), buys ordinary homes and converts them into affordable houses for people with special needs. Hello Housing snatches up real estate and turns out redesigned houses much faster than the community development organization for which Mardie worked in the Fifth Ward, in large part because Mardie has figured out a way to attract capital. Hello Housing manages loans in the tens of millions or more—sums that would have panicked the young woman who was once so worried about money that she needed a mouth guard.

Hello Housing's design process is exacting. The interiors must be constructed from healthy, nontoxic materials. They must meet the needs of the clients, many of whom require wheelchair ramps, precise climate control, or emergency power systems to keep equipment going in case the power fails. Finally, they must be beautiful. Mardie's vision is to create homes that anyone would be excited to live in.

It takes a tremendous amount of work to settle clients into their new homes. The process starts with acclimation. On a typical Saturday, a caretaker drives a client to a pretty residential enclave in the San Francisco Bay Area. Most of the homes were originally built in the 1960s and 1970s. They are simple, one-story houses with wood siding and concrete stoops. At the far end of one of the blocks sits a house the same shape and size as the others. In place of a stoop, this house has a ramp to the front door, which is painted a muted purple, perhaps, or pumpkin orange. Mardie chooses the front doors of all Hello Housing houses herself. Selecting them is her way of saying, "Welcome."

Inside, natural light streams over polished bamboo floors. The kitchen offers plenty of low, wide counters and a sink big enough to wash dishes comfortably.

Over the course of a few months, the new resident will have lunch in the house, spend the night occasionally, and finally move in. The long process pays off. Most residents find that being in their own, custom-made space is transformative—and their friends and family are equally thrilled.

Unfortunately, their neighbors are sometimes not as enthusiastic. Mardie

often attends meetings with homeowners who are angry at the thought of having disabled people move in next door. In some ways, the conversations Mardie has about integrated housing for disabled people echo the conversations her mother had with the PTA about desegregating schools. Future neighbors say things like, "We won't have to see them, will we?" and "Can you promise they'll be bedridden so they won't be on the sidewalks?"

During these meetings, Mardie and her staff take a deep breath and visualize wearing Teflon suits so the bitter remarks will slide right off them. For

tough conference calls, they all put on "power rings" purchased at the drugstore—brightly colored rubber rings filled with blinking LED lights.

These moments of solidarity with her staff are especially important because Mardie doesn't get to interact with many of the clients herself. Every now and then, she misses the relationships she had with the residents in the Fifth Ward, who came to the office for lunch sometimes or attended community picnics. Mardie's job as a founder and director of an organization is totally different. She's managing the money, the contracts, the

who refused to part with his backpack wherever he went in the institution, but who left his backpack on the porch when he learned he had his own room; or one of Mardie's favorites: within a month of moving, a ninety-year-old woman who was not verbal, apart from a few curse words, summoned her caregiver and whispered forcefully, "Thank God for my beautiful home."

The stories that Mardie finds particularly poignant are those about the impact the homes have on families. So many parents and family members dreaded going to the institution, but they look forward to visiting their loved ones in their houses. It's pleasant to sit at a dining room table together, they say, eating or drawing or just talking. One brother had not seen his sister for over five years; visiting Agnews was too painful. Now, he drops by to visit his sister nearly every day.

The ability to impact so many people's lives is the result of Mardie's hustle. Now that she's found the sweet spot in her Venn diagram, she can visualize how her work ripples outward. As the Rilke poem framed above her bed says, "I live my life in widening circles that reach out across the world. I may not complete the last one, but I give myself to it."

risk, the relationships, the process, and the organization itself. Instead of getting satisfaction from feeling like part of a community, her reward comes from the conviction that what her organization does is good for people.

Nearly every week, Mardie hears a new story about one of the residents. Like the one of a young woman with cerebral palsy who practiced walking across her own living room after moving into her new home; or the one of a man

SOCHEATA
STANDING UP AND BEING RECOGNIZED

After *New Year Baby* aired on television, Socheata was invited every few weeks to speak at a film festival or a college. She answered the audience's questions about the Khmer Rouge, and she explained what she knew about what was currently happening in Cambodia. One time she went to Long Beach, California, which has one of the largest populations of Cambodians in the United States. There, a woman took her aside.

"You know, what you did is really valuable," the woman said. "We need to videotape survivors' stories. They're getting older; their memories are fading. And look, you're a filmmaker. You should do it."

Socheata's first instinct was to say, "That isn't my project." It was the same impulse she'd had when her classmate saw her weeding the lawn and called her name—she wanted to disappear. Being singled out as someone special didn't appeal to her, nor did trying to rally other people around a cause. It seemed like too big of a risk. To be polite, she told the woman she'd think about it.

Over the next few weeks, the idea started to make sense. Speaking in public about the Khmer Rouge gave Socheata some insight into what her parents and other survivors must have felt when they described what had happened to them. It took courage to tell the story, especially for those still afraid of what might happen to them if they spoke up.

Socheata realized that if more people talked about their memories, other families could start to heal, as hers had. Collecting these stories would also give the public a repository of firsthand information about an episode in history that was at risk of being forgotten. When she really thought about it, Socheata couldn't imagine a better use for her life or her skills. Her family had already been through the worst experience possible. What did she have to lose? Even if she risked her job, her money, and her reputation, she believed that trying to make a difference in the lives of others would be worth it.

• • •

In 2007, Socheata began Khmer Legacies, a video archive in which younger generations of Cambodians interview their parents, grandparents, aunts, uncles, and other survivors of the Cambodian genocide. The oral histories give people Socheata's age and younger a chance to learn about their past, and they give older

people permission to tell their stories and, possibly, the chance to heal.

New Year Baby opened a new world to Socheata. She's partnering with schools to use the film to teach students about the Cambodian genocide, and she's working with museums to include the video testimonies of other survivors in their archives. As a result, the Cambodian genocide is coming out of the shadows. It's showing up in the historical record, and children are beginning to learn about it as they do the Vietnam War and the Holocaust.

Tucked in the back of Socheata's file cabinet in her office at Yale University's Genocide Studies program is a manila envelope with family memorabilia she used in the film: black-and-white photos of her mother's first wedding, her father's plane ticket from the refugee camp to the United States, a picture of her grandparents. She's content to leave them filed away. The artifacts are part of her life, but she recognizes that they're not all of her life. She's still more American than Cambodian, and most of her identity comes from the choices she's made for herself.

Her parents were at first skeptical that she could turn a film about their family into a career. They didn't know where the money would come from, or the job security. But, like other changemakers, Socheata has figured out ways to make it work. Her salary from grants and speaking fees isn't extravagant, but it's enough, and she's further rewarded by doing work that matters deeply to her.

Socheata's professional journey began at home. Through the process of exploring her family's history, she ultimately discovered a connection to a meaningful social issue. What began as a personal quest has expanded to become a project with tremendous social impact. The word *hustle* probably makes you think of energy or motion, but for Socheata, hustle is about quietly owning her power and grace. Every time she steps in front of hundreds of people or supports the healing that comes with speaking out, she demonstrates her commitment to show up fully rather than disappear into the shadows.

Every day she questions herself, not to tear herself down, but rather to build herself up. *What am I doing to change the community?* she demands. *What risks can I take? How can I be even bolder?*

BOLD Qs

WHEN HAVE YOU FELT "IN THE ZONE," LIKE YOU WERE DOING EXACTLY WHAT YOU SHOULD BE DOING?

_____

_____

_____

_____

_____

_____

_____

_____

_____

_____

YOUR PATH TO BOLDNESS

Heart + Head = Hustle is a framework you can use throughout your life to create a career with impact. The more reflective you are, and the more you pay attention to your feelings and thoughts, the bigger the payoff.

Keep asking yourself questions: *What social footprint do I want to make? What is my issue or cause to own? What road do I want to take, and why is this the path I'm drawn to? Why do you do what you do?*

Even if you don't have all the answers now, starting your professional life with this level of self-awareness is a real service to yourself. When you identify the causes and problems you care about most, you'll be able to recognize the opportunity to sync your heart and head and commit to the right path when you find it.

The changemakers in this book acknowledge that syncing their hearts and heads has brought them not only professional satisfaction, but personal fulfillment. Andrew is happy, Cheryl proud, Mark focused, Mardie energized, and Socheata coureagous. Their fulfillment is the fuel they use to hustle. It gives them the energy and determination to continue to work hard and well toward their goals.

In the end, society benefits from their work, and society is all of us. Choose to *be bold* and to create a meaningful life, because this path will make you happy, and because you can have an impact. The world needs you.

AFTERWORD

When I was growing up in the South Bronx in the 1960s, I knew what I wanted to do with my life: serve my community, which was devastated by poverty, violence, and a horrible education system. I had never seen anyone doing this work. I knew about lawyers and doctors and teachers and merchants, but I knew nothing of nonprofits and service. Teaching appealed to me, but I wanted to figure out a way to make a difference to an entire community, not just to one classroom.

Geoffrey Canada, Harlem Children's Zone

While I didn't know exactly how I would help my community, I was driven by a sense of service and a desire to give back. I recognized that I needed to get a good education and to really learn a set of skills so that "giving back" wasn't just a theoretical set of beliefs but a very practical strategy.

After college and graduate school, like many young people, I took whatever jobs I could find that were in my fields of expertise. Because I had chosen something I love—helping and serving—each of the jobs I found was terrific. I loved being a teacher. I loved being a principal. I loved being a program director. And I love being the CEO of Harlem Children's Zone.

My friends and family members work in all kinds of professions. Some of them love their careers, and others don't. To some of them, a job is something they *have* to go to. They're thrilled when it's Friday and unhappy when Monday comes around. They go about their work with determination and professionalism but not with the sense of joy that I have felt each day that I have worked in my chosen profession. That is what this book is all about: working with purpose, working with joy.

In the twenty-eight years I have worked at Harlem Children's Zone, I have been excited and thrilled by my job every single day. It certainly can be tiring, and at times I am glad when Friday arrives, but I am always eager to rejoin the mission on Monday. As I have often explained to my students, the perfect job is one you would do without pay.

The work I do at Harlem Children's Zone is something I would do for free. I think it's wonderful that I get paid to do it. I never imagined that one could have a career—and a successful career—helping one's community.

There are some people who don't feel the urgent need to give back, and that is fine. There are plenty of careers they can gravitate toward and do well in. But people who do feel this urge to give back should take a very hard and serious look at opportunities in the social sector. It can offer you a lifetime of service and giving, combined with adventure and the opportunity to work with some brilliant, good-hearted colleagues, and all that provides you with an opportunity to live a truly fulfilling life.

GEOFFREY CANADA, in his nearly thirty years with the nonprofit organization Harlem Children's Zone, has become nationally recognized for his pioneering work helping children and families in Harlem and as a passionate advocate for education reform. Since 1990, Canada has served as the president and CEO of the organization, which targets a 97-block area, providing an interlocking network of education, social service, and community-building programs. Harlem Children's Zone now serves over 8,800 at-risk children, from birth through college.

ACKNOWLEDGMENTS

When I began developing Echoing Green's first book, *Be Bold*, I didn't know a thing about publishing. All I knew was that we at Echoing Green had a message we wanted to shout out to the world. By following the incredible advice of a handful of champions, we got that message onto paper and into your hands.

Several years later, we looked up and had more to say. We approached the development of *Work on Purpose* with our eyes wide open and surrounded ourselves with the absolute best supporters. It was through their generous counsel that my team and I were able to create this book.

First and foremost, thank you to Kelly Nuxoll, my partner in writing this book. When Kelly signed up for this journey, she didn't know how many twisting roads awaited her—but she navigated every one with grace and a can-do attitude. Partners from the beginning, we weren't surprised when we began showing up to meetings wearing similar clothes and finishing each other's sentences. It's been a wonderful voyage.

Thank you to the five outstanding Echoing Green Fellows: Andrew Youn, Cheryl Dorsey, Mark Hanis, Mardie Oakes, and Socheata Poeuv. You revealed untold parts of your stories to show that meaningful, impact-driven careers are not something handed to the lucky ones but something everyone can work to achieve. The more I partnered with you, the more strongly I was convinced that stories like yours have to be told. I continue to draw inspiration from the examples you set.

All of us at Echoing Green are grateful to Lance Armstrong, Doug Ulman, and Geoffrey Canada for authoring sections of this book. Your lives provide stellar examples of impact, and we are humbled that you became part of our mission to help others build purpose-driven careers.

A sincere, boisterous "Thank you!" to Dan Weiss, beloved Echoing Green board member, book publishing whiz, and mentor, whose no-nonsense advice is the reason this book came together. And much appreciation to Emma Chastain, our editor, whose obsession with clarity and ability to rework a paragraph are magical.

Thank you to our supporters, especially the David Weekley Family Foundation, the Edwin Gould Foundation, and The Pershing Square Foundation. Without all of your support, this book would not be possible. A special note of appreciation to the W.K. Kellogg Foundation for its support of *Be Bold* and *Work on Purpose*. Thank you to Tom Reis of the Kellogg Foundation, who was the first person to have faith in this idea, and believed that this project could become a reality.

Thank you to the Echoing Green staff and interns, who believe deeply in this project and worked tirelessly to bring it to fruition. Special thanks to Hannah Alexander, who developed and managed this project, and who was never intimidated by the mile-long to-do lists. And many thanks to Mailande Moran and Zachary Kolodin for their early work on the book.

We couldn't have published this book without the incredible assistance of: Tony Deifell, whose photos capture the souls of our protagonists (and literally take my breath away); Kelly Blair, our world-class designer; Jessi Arrington of WORKSHOP for designing the front and back cover; Britt Bravo and Kathy Crutcher, who partnered with us on the Instructor's Guide; Rachel Newton Bellow, who provided early insight; and Jessica Kovler and Tony Moore for copy editing the manuscript.

My gratitude to Echoing Green president Cheryl Dorsey goes beyond words. Cheryl was the one who first recognized the potential of *Be Bold*, and she showed great boldness by plunging into the publishing process even though neither one of us knew quite what it would entail. Perhaps even more boldly, even after learning how much effort it takes to create a book, she agreed for Echoing Green to do it all over again with *Work on Purpose*. I certainly learned to *work on purpose* by working alongside Cheryl over this past decade.

I opened the book with a quote by Dag Hammarskjöld, who so eloquently said, "For all that has been, thanks. For all that will be, yes." I am thankful that we have been able to create this book, but it is what will be in the future that drives me. It's my dream that more and more people will not merely have jobs but have purpose.

RESOURCES

Here are some organizations and programs that can help you on your path.

ACADEMIC PROGRAMS

American University's Entrepreneurship MBA Concentration
www.american.edu/kogod/graduate/mbaconcentrations//entrepreneurship.cfm
Provides students with the entrepreneurial mindset, skills, and tools for multiple contexts, including starting a business and/or being an entrepreneur in corporations, nonprofit organizations, government, or international organizations.

Babson College's Arthur M. Blank Center for Entrepreneurship
www3.babson.edu/eship/aboutblank
Develops innovation in an integrated, experience-based learning environment.

Brown University's Social Innovation Initiative (SII)
www.swearercenter.brown.edu/sii
Works to inspire and support student and alumni social entrepreneurs through the creation of a community that expands critical skills, knowledge, resources, and social networks.

Columbia University's Social Enterprise Program (SEP)
www4.gsb.columbia.edu/socialenterprise
Advances the understanding of how management can contribute to society and the environment, and develops the next generation of social enterprise leaders.

Cornell University's Center for Sustainable Global Enterprise (SGE)
www2.johnson.cornell.edu/sge/index.cfm
Strives to advance the global knowledge base in sustainable enterprise and of critical knowledge and research related to business and sustainability.

Duke University's Center for the Advancement of Social Entrepreneurship (CASE)
www.caseatduke.org
Promotes the entrepreneurial pursuit of social impact through the thoughtful adaptation of business expertise.

Georgia Institute of Technology's Institute for Leadership and Entrepreneurship (ILE)
www.ile.gatech.edu/index.html
Enhances leadership and entrepreneurship for socially responsible and sustainable value creation.

Harvard University's John F. Kennedy School of Government
www.hks.harvard.edu
Prepares and trains students to be leaders in the private, public, or nonprofit sector.

Institute for Nonprofit Management (INPM)
www.inpm.pdx.edu
Offers access to both professional certificates and degree programs through Portland State University's Department of Public Administration. Works to build the nonprofit sector by teaching practical skills and encouraging lifelong learning to nonprofit professionals and volunteers.

Milano—The New School for Management and Urban Policy
www.newschool.edu/milano
Trains professionals to become effective managers and policymakers in government, business, and the nonprofit sector.

MIT's Entrepreneurship Center
entrepreneurship.mit.edu
Provides courses to design and launch successful new ventures based on innovative technologies.

New York University's Catherine B. Reynolds Foundation Program in Social Entrepreneurship
www.nyu.edu/reynolds
Attracts, encourages, and trains a new generation of leaders in public service.

Northwestern University's Social Enterprise at Kellogg (SEEK)
www.kellogg.northwestern.edu/academic/seek/index.htm
Builds leadership skills and awareness to help students be socially responsible global leaders in the business, nonprofit, and government sectors.

Pace University's Helene and Grant Wilson Center for Social Entrepreneurship
www.pace.edu/wilsoncenter
Promotes social change through entrepreneurship and furthers this mission by serving students and nonprofit organizations with education, research, communication, and advisory services.

Purdue University's Burton D. Morgan Center for Entrepreneurship (BDMCE)
www.purdue.edu/dp/entrepreneurship
Promotes a culture of entrepreneurship, with activity in both commercialization and education.

Santa Clara University's Center for Innovation and Entrepreneurship (CIE)
www.scu.edu/business/cie/about/index-new.cfm
Helps foster, promote, and strengthen entrepreneurial talent by providing networking, educational, and advisory services.

Skoll Centre for Social Entrepreneurship at the University of Oxford Saïd Business School
www.sbs.ox.ac.uk/centres/skoll
Fosters innovative social transformation through education, research, and collaboration.

Stanford Graduate School of Business's Center for Social Innovation (CSI)
csi.gsb.stanford.edu
Believes that business schools have a responsibility to teach students to be innovative, principled, and insightful leaders who can change the world. Represents a cornerstone of Stanford's multidisciplinary approach to management and leadership education.

Syracuse University's Department of Entrepreneurship and Emerging Enterprises (EEE)
whitman.syr.edu/Academics/EEE
Helps students discover their innate entrepreneurial potential and gives them a set of tools and perspectives to capitalize on that potential.

University of California Berkeley's Lester Center for Entrepreneurship
entrepreneurship.berkeley.edu
Inspires students and colleagues to create new ventures, discover new sources of value, and change the world for the better.

University of California Los Angeles's Harold and Pauline Price Center for Entrepreneurial Studies
www.anderson.ucla.edu/price.xml
Fosters the study and practice of entrepreneurship and business innovation by providing the foundation on which creativity can flourish and individuals can succeed.

University of Florida's Center for Entrepreneurship and Innovation (CEI)
warrington.ufl.edu/fire/entrepreneurship/cei
Provides students with the tools and experiences necessary to creatively pursue new opportunities and innovations in the start-up, social, and corporate venture arenas.

University of Michigan's Nonprofit and Public Management Center (NPM)
nonprofit.umich.edu
Equips future leaders in the private, public and nonprofit sectors with interdisciplinary insight that can help them operate more effectively when working for or collaborating with nonprofit and public institutions.

University of North Carolina's Center for Sustainable Enterprise (CSE)
www.kenan-flagler.unc.edu/cse
Helps executives and future business leaders understand how social and environmental considerations are changing the competitive landscape of business.

University of Notre Dame's Center for Social Concerns (CSC)
socialconcerns.nd.edu
Provides educational experiences in social concerns and acts as the service-and community-based learning hub of the University of Notre Dame.

University of Portland's Center for Entrepreneurship
www.up.edu/cfe
Aims to foster the creation of new business ventures and to develop existing enterprises.

University of Virginia's Batten Institute

www.batteninstitute.org

Creates knowledge about the transformative power of entrepreneurship and innovation toward the cultivation of principled, entrepreneurial leaders.

Yale University's Program on Social Enterprise (PSE)

pse.som.yale.edu

Supports scholars, students, alumni, and practitioners interested in exploring the ways in which business skills and disciplines can be harnessed to most effectively and efficiently achieve social objectives.

CAREER & INTERNSHIPS

Bridgestar

www.bridgestar.org

Provides a free nonprofit management job board, content, and tools designed to help nonprofit organizations build strong leadership teams and individuals pursue career paths as nonprofit leaders.

Careers In Nonprofits

www.careersinnonprofits.com

Connects the best people with the best causes. Serving Chicago, Los Angeles, San Francisco, and Washington, D.C., has extensive networks of connections and strategic partnerships with nonprofit organizations.

Charity Village

www.charityvillage.com

Provides an online source of information, news, jobs, services, and resources for the Canadian nonprofit community.

Commongood Careers

www.cgcareers.org

Enables innovative nonprofits to build strong organizations through the recruitment, retention, and development of outstanding talent.

Craigslist

www.craigslist.org

Features city-specific classified ads, forums, and job listings in many categories, including nonprofit.

DotOrgJobs.com

www.dotorgjobs.com

Lists nonprofit jobs, which are searchable by category, location, and experience level.

Idealist.org

www.idealist.org

Gives people and organizations a place online to exchange resources and ideas, locate opportunities and supporters, and take steps toward building a world where all people can lead free and dignified lives.

Jobs for Change

jobs.change.org

Seeks to spark a nationwide movement toward careers in the nonprofit, government, and social enterprise sectors.

Justmeans

www.justmeans.com

Aims to extend messages concerning social causes and the environment to the right companies and people in order to drive engagement through interaction, incentives, and rewards.

On-Ramps

www.on-ramps.com

Helps organizations recruit the best talent available, no matter the function or sector.

Opportunity Knocks

www.opportunityknocks.org

Provides a national online job site, HR resource, and career development destination focused exclusively on the nonprofit community. Leads and supports efforts that help further nonprofit careers and promote a robust workforce that enables organizations to complete their missions.

CIVIC ENGAGEMENT, VOLUNTEERING, & PUBLIC SERVICE ORGANIZATIONS

AmeriCorps

www.americorps.gov

Offers more than 75,000 opportunities for adults of all

ages and backgrounds to serve through a network of partnerships with local and national nonprofit groups.

Arsalyn

www.arsalyn.org/Search.asp

Provides an ever-growing database of youth civic and political organizations.

AVODAH: The Jewish Service Corps

www.avodah.net

Engages young people in direct work on the causes and effects of poverty in the United States.

Campus Compact

www.compact.org

Promotes community service, civic engagement, and service learning in higher education, as a national coalition of more than 1,100 college and university presidents, representing some 6 million students.

Citizen Corps

www.citizencorps.gov

Provides opportunities for people to participate in a range of measures to make their families, their homes, and their communities safer from the threats of crime, terrorism, and disasters of all kinds.

Citizens for Global Solutions

www.globalsolutions.org

Works to build political will in the United States to achieve a future in which nations work together to abolish war, protect human rights and freedoms, and solve the problems facing humanity that no nation can solve alone.

City Year

www.cityyear.org

Unites young people of all backgrounds for a year of full-time service, giving them skills and opportunities to change the world.

Design Corps

www.designcorps.org

Creates positive change in communities by providing architecture and planning services.

HandsOn Network

www.handsonnetwork.org

Inspires, equips, and mobilizes people to change lives through service.

Hip Hop Caucus

www.hiphopcaucus.org

Fosters civic engagement among young people of color on issues of social and economic justice, human rights, the environment, and international peace, so they can attain increased opportunities for themselves and their communities.

LIFT

www.liftcommunities.org

Combats poverty and expands opportunities for all people in the United States.

Partnership for Public Service

www.ourpublicservice.org

Works to revitalize our federal government by inspiring a new generation to serve and by transforming the way government works.

Points of Light Institute

www.pointsoflight.org

Inspires, equips, and mobilizes people to take action that changes the world.

Public Allies

www.publicallies.org

Advances new leadership to strengthen communities, nonprofits, and civic participation.

Serve.gov

www.serve.gov

Enables individuals to not only find volunteer opportunities in their community but also to create their own.

Servenet.org

www.servenet.org

Enables youth volunteers to connect with local nonprofits to make a difference in their communities throughout the United States.

ServiceNation

www.servicenation.org

Increases service opportunities and elevates service as a core ideal and problem-solving strategy in American society.

Teach For America

www.teachforamerica.org

Builds the movement to eliminate educational

inequity by enlisting America's most promising future leaders in the effort.

VolunteerMatch

www.volunteermatch.org

Strengthens communities by making it easier for good people and good causes to connect. Offers a variety of online services to support a community of nonprofit, volunteer, and business leaders committed to civic engagement.

YouthBuild

www.youthbuild.org

Addresses core issues facing low-income communities: housing, education, employment, crime prevention, and leadership development. Enables low-income young people ages sixteen to twenty-four to work toward their GEDs or high school diplomas, learn job skills, and serve their communities by building affordable housing and transform their own lives and roles in society.

Youth Service America (YSA)

www.ysa.org

Partners with thousands of organizations in more than 100 countries to expand the impact of the youth service movement with families, communities, schools, corporations, and governments.

HIGH SCHOOL & UNDERGRADUATE FELLOWSHIPS & AWARDS

Corella and Bertram F. Bonner Foundation

www.bonner.org

Seeks to improve the lives of individuals and communities by helping meet the basic needs of nutrition and educational opportunity through sustained partnerships with colleges and congregations.

Girls for a Change (GFC)

www.girlsforachange.org

Empowers thousands of teen girls to create and lead social change. Provides girls with professional female role models, leadership training, and the inspiration to work together in teams to solve persistent societal problems in their communities.

Nonprofit Leadership Alliance (formerly American Humanics)

www.humanics.org

Educates, prepares, and certifies professionals to strengthen and lead nonprofit organizations, as a national alliance of colleges, universities, and nonprofit organizations.

Posse Foundation

www.possefoundation.org

Identifies public high school students with extraordinary academic and leadership potential who may be overlooked by traditional college selection processes for four-year, full-tuition leadership scholarship awards.

Public Policy and International Affairs Fellowship Program (PPIA)

www.ppiaprogram.org

Prepares young adults for advanced degrees and ultimately for careers and influential roles serving the public good.

Thomas J. Watson Foundation

www.watsonfellowship.org

Offers college graduates of "unusual promise" a year of independent, purposeful exploration and travel—in international settings new to them—to enhance their capacity for resourcefulness, imagination, openness, and leadership, and to foster their humane and effective participation in the world community.

Youth Venture

www.genv.net

Invests in young people who want to launch sustainable ventures that create lasting benefit to their communities and then connects them to a global network of like-minded youth.

GRADUATE-LEVEL & EARLY-STAGE CAREER FELLOWSHIPS & AWARDS

Bernard L. Schwartz Fellows Program

fellows.newamerica.net

Awards fellowships to original thinkers eager to

advance a better understanding of policy challenges facing our society.

Coro

www.coro.org

Prepares individuals for effective and ethical leadership in the public affairs arena.

The Fellowship for Emerging Leaders in Public Service (FELPS)

wagner.nyu.edu/leadership/leadership_dev/felps

Inspires, engages, and connects emerging public service leaders with a unique career planning and professional development opportunity. Recognizes the strong commitment to public service that fellows have demonstrated and strengthens this commitment by providing professional development and networking opportunities aimed at assisting fellows in developing plans for successful public service careers.

Open Society Fellowship

www.soros.org/initiatives/fellowship

Supports individuals seeking innovative and unconventional approaches to fundamental open-society challenges. Funds work that will enrich public understanding of those challenges and stimulate far-reaching and probing conversations within the Open Society Institute and across the world.

Paul and Phyllis Fireman Public Service Fellowship at City Year

haas-fmp.stanford.edu/fellowship.php?ef_id=369&

Unites young people of all backgrounds for a year of full-time service, giving them the skills and opportunities to change the world.

Public Policy and International Affairs Fellowship Program (PPIA)

www.ppiaprogram.org

Prepares young adults for an advanced degree and ultimately for careers and influential roles serving the public good. Focuses on students from groups who are underrepresented in leadership positions in government, nonprofits, international organizations, and other institutional settings.

National Grid's Samuel Huntington Public Service Award

www.nationalgridus.com/masselectric/about_us/award.asp

Provides a stipend for a graduating college senior to pursue one year of public service anywhere in the world before proceeding on to graduate school or a career.

StartingBloc

www.startingbloc.org

Educates, inspires, and connects emerging leaders to drive social innovation across sectors.

Strongheart Fellowship Program

www.strongheartfellowship.org

Helps bright, resilient young people from extremely challenging circumstances around the globe develop into compassionate, innovative problem-solvers and leaders that can affect significant social change.

The Urban Fellows Program

www.nyc.gov/html/dcas/html/employment/urbanfellows.shtml

Provides an opportunity for young professionals to gain meaningful work experience in public policy, urban planning, and government operations as they consider careers in public service.

INTERNATIONAL CIVIC ENGAGEMENT & VOLUNTEERING PROGRAMS

AIESEC

www.aiesec.org

Provides a platform for youth leadership development and offers young people the opportunity to be global citizens, to change the world, and to get experience and skills that matter today.

Altrusa International

www.altrusa.com

Provides community service, develops leadership, fosters international understanding, and encourages fellowship, as an international network of executives and professionals in diversified career classifications.

Atlas Service Corps

www.atlascorps.org

Develops leaders, strengthens organizations, and promotes innovation through an overseas fellowship of skilled professionals.

Global Citizen Year (GCY)

globalcitizenyear.org

Builds a movement of young Americans who engage in a transformative "bridge year" between high school and college. Creates opportunities for emerging leaders to work as apprentices around the world through an innovative cross-sector model that partners with international NGOs and high schools and colleges in the United States.

Habitat for Humanity International

www.habitat.org

Seeks to eliminate poverty housing and homelessness from the world and to make decent shelter a matter of conscience.

Institute of International Education (IIE)

www.iie.org

Fosters mutual understanding, develops global leaders, and protects academic freedom worldwide through educational exchange and training programs.

International Partnership for Service-Learning and Leadership (IPSL)

www.ipsl.org

Integrates academic studies with volunteer service and full cultural immersion to give students a deeper, more meaningful study-abroad experience.

Peace Corps

www.peacecorps.gov

Shares with the world America's most precious resource: its people. Collaborates with local community members in seventy-four countries in Africa, Asia, the Caribbean, Central and South America, Europe, and the Middle East in areas like education, youth outreach, community development, the environment, and information technology.

Service for Peace (SFP)

www.serviceforpeace.org

Provides service and learning opportunities through community projects, which promote transformational and sustainable personal and community development around the world.

World Volunteer Web

www.worldvolunteerweb.org

Serves as a global clearinghouse for information and resources linked to volunteerism that can be used for campaigning, advocacy, and networking.

Worldwide Helpers (WWH)

www.worldwidehelpers.org

Fosters partnerships between volunteers and charitable organizations worldwide and commits itself to removing the financial barriers of volunteering by providing only low/no-cost projects.

MEDIA & BLOGS

A. Fine Blog

afine2.wordpress.com

Explores the use of social media tools for social change.

Beth's Blog: How Nonprofits Can Use Social Media to Power Social Networks for Change

www.bethkanter.org

Blogs about nonprofits, social media, and strategy.

Care2

www.care2.com

Uses the power of business to make a positive social and earth-friendly impact on the world.

Causecast

www.causecast.org

Provides an online platform where users can explore issues and causes, and connect with people wanting to make a difference.

Change.org

www.change.org

Raises awareness about important causes and empowers people to take action with leading nonprofits.

Chronicle of Philanthropy

philanthropy.com

Provides news, in print and online, for charity leaders, fundraisers, grant makers, and other people involved in the philanthropic enterprise.

Dowser
dowser.org

Reports on social innovation, focusing on the question, "Who is solving what, and how?" Highlights creative approaches to social change to help people understand how to build better communities and a better world.

Future Leaders in Philanthropy (FLiP)
www.networkflip.com

Creates a community and a network where future leaders can meet, learn, exchange ideas, and contribute to each other's success.

GOOD
www.good.is

Provides content, experiences, and utilities to serve the community.

Have Fun, Do Good
havefundogood.blogspot.com

Blogs for people who want to make the world a better place and have fun.

Katya's Nonprofit Marketing Blog
www.nonprofitmarketingblog.com

A personal blog on Robin Hood marketing—the concept of stealing corporate savvy to sell just causes—and Katya's life as a marketer, from Washington, D.C., to Madagascar, to points in between.

Next Billion
www.nextbillion.net

Brings together a community of business leaders, social entrepreneurs, NGOs, policymakers, and academics who want to explore the connection between development and enterprise.

SIX (Social Innovation eXchange)
www.socialinnovationexchange.org

Promotes social innovation and growing the capacity of the field in a global community of over 700 individuals and organizations—including small NGOs and global firms, public agencies, and academics.

Social Edge
www.socialedge.org

Provides a global online community where social

entrepreneurs and other practitioners of the social benefit sector connect to network, learn, inspire, and share resources.

Social ROI
www.socialroi.com

Enables social entrepreneurship and spreads the word about some of the good stuff that's happening in the space.

Spare Change
blog.social-marketing.com

Uses social marketing to promote health and social issues for nonprofits and public agencies at Weinrich Communications.

Stanford Social Innovation Review (SSIR)
www.ssireview.org

Shares substantive insights and practical experiences that will help those who do the important work of improving society to do it even better.

TakePart
www.takepart.com

Connects its members directly to the issues that inspire them to engage, contribute, and take action.

Wild Apricot Blog
www.wildapricot.com/blogs/newsblog

Discusses issues and trends in web technologies for nonprofits—charities, associations, clubs, and other organizations.

WorldChanging
www.worldchanging.com

Covers innovative solutions to the planet's problems and inspires readers around the world with stories of new tools, models, and ideas for building a bright, green future.

NETWORKING & MEMBERSHIP ORGANIZATIONS

85 Broads
www.85broads.com

Aims to build a multigenerational global network of ambitious, intelligent women who want to inspire each other to blaze new trails, scale new heights, and achieve a life of true significance.

Craigslist Foundation
www.craigslistfoundation.org
Empowers people to strengthen their communities by connecting them to the resources they need to effectively engage in community building.

Emerging Practitioners in Philanthropy (EPIP)
www.epip.org
Strengthens the next generation of grant makers to advance effective social justice philanthropy.

Independent Sector
www.independentsector.org
Advances the common good in America and around the world.

National Council of Nonprofits
www.councilofnonprofits.org
Links local nonprofit organizations across the nation through state associations. Helps small and midsize nonprofits manage and lead more effectively, collaborate and exchange solutions, engage in critical policy issues affecting the sector, and achieve greater impact in their communities.

Net Impact
www.netimpact.org
Uses the power of business to create a more socially and environmentally sustainable world.

Social Venture Network (SVN)
www.svn.org
Builds a just and sustainable world through socially and environmentally sustainable business, as a network of socially responsible business leaders.

Women's Funding Network (WFN)
www.womensfundingnetwork.org
Invests in women's solutions across the globe, as one of the largest collaborative philanthropic networks in the world.

Young Nonprofit Professionals Network (YNPN)
www.ynpn.org
Engages and supports future nonprofit and

community leaders through professional development, networking, and social opportunities.

Young Women Social Entrepreneurs (YWSE)
www.ywse.org
Serves women with a socially conscious agenda who are founders and leaders within businesses, nonprofits, and government organizations.

RESOURCES FOR NONPROFIT & SOCIAL SECTOR ORGANIZATIONS

Alliance for Nonprofit Management
www.allianceonline.org
Improves the management and governance capacity of nonprofits, as a professional association of individuals and organizations.

BoardSource
www.boardsource.org
Advances the public good by building exceptional nonprofit boards and inspiring board service.

The Bridgespan Group
www.bridgespan.org
Helps nonprofit and philanthropic leaders develop strategies and build organizations that inspire and accelerate social change.

The Case Foundation
www.casefoundation.org
Expands giving, promotes everyday philanthropy, deepens civic engagement, and broadens the use of new technologies to make giving more informed, efficient, and effective.

Foundation Center
foundationcenter.org
Connects nonprofits and the grant makers supporting them to tools they can use and information they can trust.

Google for Nonprofits
www.google.com/nonprofits
Provides an informational website that offers tips and

guidance on how nonprofits can use Google to promote their work, raise funds, and operate more efficiently.

Open Society Institute (OSI)

www.soros.org

Seeks to shape public policies that assure greater fairness in political, legal, and economic systems and safeguard fundamental rights.

The Resource Alliance

www.resource-alliance.org

Builds the fundraising capabilities of the nonprofit sector worldwide.

TechSoup

home.techsoup.org

Offers nonprofits a one-stop resource for technology needs by providing free information, resources, and support.

USA.gov for Nonprofits

www.usa.gov/Business/Nonprofit.shtml

Provides links to federal funding and grant opportunities, tax information, and management and operations resources for nonprofits.

World Association of Non-Governmental Organizations (WANGO)

www.wango.org

Provides the mechanism and support needed for NGOs to connect, partner, share, inspire, and multiply their contributions to solve humanity's basic problems.

SOCIAL ENTREPRENEURSHIP GRANT MAKERS/FELLOWSHIPS

Ashoka

www.ashoka.org

Provides a global association of the world's leading social entrepreneurs—men and women with system-changing solutions for the world's most urgent social problems.

Breakthrough

www.breakthroughfund.org.uk

Provides funding and management support to help established U.K. social enterprises scale up and maximize their social impact.

Clinton Global Initiative University (CGI U)

www.cgiu.org

Gives Outstanding Commitment Awards, which are grants to exceptional students who have made Commitments to Action that address social or environmental challenges on campuses, in communities, or in different parts of the world.

Do Something

www.dosomething.org/grants

Gives micro-grants to young people pursuing sustainable community action projects and programs.

Draper Richards Kaplan Foundation

www.draperrichards.org

Provides selected social entrepreneurs with funding of $100,000 annually for three years specifically and solely for entrepreneurs starting new nonprofit organizations.

Echoing Green

www.echoinggreen.org

Unleashes next generation talent to solve the world's biggest problems.

Impetus Trust

www.impetus.org.uk

Invests in innovative U.K. charities and social enterprises fighting economic disadvantage in the U.K. and internationally.

Mobilize.org

www.mobilize.org

Provides seed funding to emerging civic entrepreneurs.

New Profit

www.newprofit.com

Helps innovative social entrepreneurs and their organizations dramatically improve opportunities for children, families, and communities.

Nonprofit Enterprise and Self-sustainability Team (NESsT)

www.nesst.org

Works to solve critical problems in emerging-market countries by developing and supporting enterprises that strengthen civil society organizations' financial sustainability and maximize their social impact.

Rainer Arnhold Fellows Program
www.rainerfellows.org
Supports social entrepreneurs with particularly promising solutions to health, poverty, and conservation issues in the developing world.

Sparkseed
www.sparkseed.org
Invests in young social entrepreneurs of tomorrow as they lead social ventures today. Provides guidance, funding, and tools to college students who will change the world.

UnLtd, the Foundation for Social Entrepreneurs
www.unltd.org.uk
Supports social entrepreneurs in the U.K.

Unreasonable Institute
unreasonableinstitute.org
Aims to incubate and finance thousands of social ventures that will each effectively address a major global issue, become financially self-sustaining within a year, scale beyond the country of origin within three years, and ultimately reach at least 1 million people.

The Young Foundation
www.youngfoundation.org.uk
Brings together insight, innovation, and entrepreneurship to meet social needs. Works across the U.K. and internationally, carrying out research, influencing policy, creating new organizations, and supporting others to do the same, often with imaginative uses of new technology.

THOUGHT LEADERSHIP ORGANIZATIONS

America's Promise Alliance
www.americaspromise.org
Improves lives and changes outcomes for children through a cross-sector partnership of more than 400 corporations, nonprofits, faith-based organizations, and advocacy groups.

Brookings Institution
www.brookings.edu
Conducts high-quality, independent research and, based on that research, provides innovative, practical recommendations that advance three broad goals:

strengthen American democracy; foster the economic and social welfare, security, and opportunity of all Americans; and secure a more open, safe, prosperous, and cooperative international system.

Leader to Leader Institute
www.leadertoleader.org
Strengthens the leadership of the social sector by providing social sector leaders with essential leadership wisdom, inspiration, and resources to lead for innovation and to build vibrant social sector organizations.

PopTech
www.poptech.org
Hosts a one-of-a-kind conference, a community of remarkable people, and an ongoing conversation about science, technology, and the future of ideas.

TED (Technology, Entertainment, Design)
www.ted.com
Hosts annual conferences in Long Beach, CA, and Oxford, U.K., bringing together the world's most fascinating thinkers and doers, who are challenged to give the talk of their lives.

TRAINING & LEADERSHIP DEVELOPMENT

American Majority
www.americanmajority.org
Trains and equips a national network of leadership committed to individual freedom through limited government and the free market.

The Aspen Institute
www.aspeninstitute.org
Fosters values-based leadership and encourages individuals to reflect on the ideals and ideas that define a good society, and to provide a neutral and balanced venue for discussing and acting on critical issues.

Generation Change
www.communitychange.org/our-projects/generationchange
Recruits, trains, and supports tomorrow's grassroots

organizers and leaders to confront the challenges of poverty and injustice in the 21st century.

Institute for Responsible Citizenship

www.i4rc.org

Prepares high-achieving African American men for successful careers in business, law, government, public service, education, journalism, the sciences, medicine, ministry, and the arts.

Leadership Learning Community (LLC)

www.leadershiplearning.org

Transforms the way leadership development work is conceived, conducted, and evaluated, primarily within the nonprofit sector, through a national network of hundreds of experienced funders, consultants, and leadership development programs.

Management Leadership for Tomorrow (MLT)

www.ml4t.org

Develops the next generation of African American, Hispanic, and Native American leaders in major corporations, nonprofit organizations, and entrepreneurial ventures.

The OpEd Project

www.theopedproject.org

Expands public debate, with an immediate emphasis on enlarging the pool of women experts who are accessing (and are accessible to) our nation's key print and online forums—which are a gateway into public debate, feed all other media, and are a hub of thought leadership.

Rockwood Leadership Institute

www.rockwoodfund.org

Provides individuals, organizations, and networks in the social benefit sector with powerful and effective training in leadership and collaboration.

Running Start

www.runningstartonline.org

Provides young women and girls with the skills and confidence they need to become the political leaders of tomorrow.

The White House Project

www.thewhitehouseproject.org

Aims to advance women's leadership in all communities and sectors—up to the U.S. presidency—by filling the leadership pipeline with a richly diverse, critical mass of women.

Transformative Action Institute (TAI)

www.transformativeaction.org

Trains a new generation of social entrepreneurs, innovators, visionaries, and problem solvers for the 21st century.

YOUTH & STUDENT ORGANIZATIONS

Americans for Informed Democracy (AID)

www.aidemocracy.org

Empowers and equips young people in the United States to address global issues—poverty, health, climate change, peace, and security—through raising awareness and actions that promote just and sustainable solutions on their campuses, in their communities, and nationally.

Bus Federation

www.busfederation.com

Engages the next generation of voters and leaders, mobilizing thousands of volunteers for political action and civic engagement.

Campus Progress

www.campusprogress.org

Acts to empower new progressive leaders nationwide as they develop fresh ideas, communicate in new ways, push policy outcomes in a progressive direction, and build a strong progressive movement.

Declare Yourself

www.declareyourself.com

Empowers and encourages every eligible eighteen-to-twenty-nine-year-old in America to register and vote in local and national elections.

Global Citizen Corps (GCC)

www.globalcitizencorps.org

Houses a movement of youth who think and act globally, have the passion to build a better world, and are committed to ending global poverty.

The Global Fund for Children (GFC)

www.globalfundforchildren.org

Provides capital to strengthen innovative

community-based organizations serving the most vulnerable children and youth.

Global Youth Action Network (GYAN)
gyan.tigweb.org
Unites the efforts of young people working to improve our world.

National Society of Leadership and Success
www.societyleadership.org
Offers life-changing lectures from the nation's leading presenters and a community where like-minded, success-oriented individuals come together to learn from and help one another succeed.

Project Pericles
www.projectpericles.org
Encourages and facilitates commitments by colleges and universities to include social responsibility and participatory citizenship as essential elements of their educational programs.

Rock the Vote
www.rockthevote.com
Engages and builds the political power of young people to achieve progressive change in the United States. Uses music, popular culture, and new technologies to engage and incite young people to register and vote in every election and gives young people the tools to identify, learn about, and take action on the issues that affect their lives.

Roosevelt Institute Campus Network
www.rooseveltcampusnetwork.org
Engages new generations in a unique form of progressive activism that empowers young people as leaders and promotes their ideas for change as the United States' only student policy organization.

TakingITGlobal (TIG)
www.tigweb.org
Provides youth with access to global opportunities, cross-cultural connections, and meaningful participation in decision making on issues concerning young people, as an online collaborative learning community.

United States Student Association (USSA)
www.usstudents.org
Develops current and future leaders and amplifies the student voice at the local, state, and national levels by mobilizing grassroots power to win concrete victories on student issues.

ECHOING GREEN FELLOWS PROFILED IN WORK ON PURPOSE

Cheryl Dorsey

www.echoinggreen.org

Echoing Green unleashes next generation talent to
solve the world's biggest problems.

Mark Hanis

www.genocideintervention.net

Genocide Intervention Network (GI-NET) empowers
individuals and communities with the tools to prevent
and stop genocide.

On November 1, 2010, Genocide Intervention
Network and The Save Darfur Coalition merged to
create a more powerful voice dedicated to prevent-
ing and stopping large-scale, deliberate atrocities
against civilians. The merger creates the largest
anti-genocide organization that combined, boasts a
membership base of over 800,000 committed activists
globally. The merged organization's new brand and
name will be launched in the coming months.

Mardie Oakes

www.hellohousing.org

Hello Housing (formerly Hallmark Community
Solutions) works at the intersection of finance,
design, policy, and community to create affordable
housing for those most in need.

Socheata Poeuv

www.khmerlegacies.org

Khmer Legacies is creating a video history archive
about the Cambodian genocide from the perspective
of survivors. The organization aims to videotape thousands of testimonies of Cambodian survivors in which
the younger generation interviews the older generation.

Andrew Youn

www.oneacrefund.org

One Acre Fund empowers chronically hungry farm
families in East Africa to permanently lift themselves
out of hunger and poverty.

THANK YOU TO OUR SUPPORTERS

We would like to thank all of our *Work on Purpose* supporters. In particular, we would like to acknowledge the following key supporters:

DAVID WEEKLEY FAMILY FOUNDATION

The David Weekley Family Foundation is a venture philanthropy group that invests treasure, talent, and time in organizations doing the most for the least. The Foundation aims to reduce global poverty by scaling proven innovations that generate more income for the poor and that provide the poor with access to affordable education and healthcare. It also supports organizations that drive toward sustainability with deep and lasting results.

EdwinGould Foundation

The Edwin Gould Foundation invests time, money, and resources to seed and grow educational models that create effective solutions to increase the number of college graduates from under-resourced communities. The Foundation advocates nationally for strong, workable solutions and policies that help motivated yet underserved students enter college, graduate and advance society. At the same time, the Foundation demonstrates locally by partnering with a select number of educational nonprofits in the New York metropolitan area who are developing effective strategies for student success.

Founded in December 2006 by William and Karen Ackman, The Pershing Square Foundation makes leveraged grants to entrepreneurial leaders who, through their work, facilitate problem solving and change in the areas of education, global health care, human rights, poverty alleviation, and the arts.